D0364050

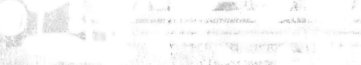

Jazz

QUADRILLE

The knowledge.
Jazz | John Fordham

Publishing consultant Jane O'Shea
Editor Romilly Morgan
Creative director Helen Lewis
Art direction & design Claire Peters
Illustrator Claire Peters
Production Vincent Smith, Tom Moore

First published in 2015 by
Quadrille Publishing
www.quadrille.co.uk

Quadrille is an imprint of Hardie Grant.
www.hardiegrant.com.au

Text © 2015 John Fordham
Design and layout © 2015
Quadrille Publishing Limited

Cataloguing in Publication Data:
a catalogue record for this book
is available from the British Library.

ISBN 978 184949 623 0

Printed in the UK

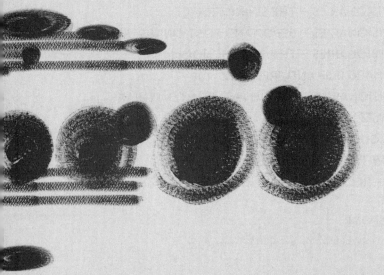

1 INTRODUCTION

I must have heard jazz long before I discovered that it had that seductive four-letter word for a name – but when I think back to my first real encounter with its free-spirited nature, magical sounds come echoing back with the intensity of all life-changing moments.

I can hear a surging rhythm, powered by the hiss of a drumstick flickering on a cymbal and the heartbeat of a deep and steady bassline, that made me want to dance for the first time in my life. I can hear a trumpet being played as if it were a seductively cajoling voice. I can hear a piano played with a strange, jarring clang, as if the notes of the chords are being crushed too close together. And I hear the entwining melodies of several musicians merging into one voice, even though there are ragged edges to the music that suggest they just thought it up as they went along. I think I fell in love with jazz because it sounded just like life, as it's lived and improvised from moment to moment: imperfect declarations of wonderment or love, fevers of anguish or anger, cool confidence in a sauntering walk, despondency in the purple tones of a slow blues.

Jazz is sometimes thought of as a music of the past, preserved only in the affections of a devoted cognoscenti. The reason for that is not difficult to unearth. Jazz was once the world's pop music, from the 1920s' Jazz Age to the years of the swing craze that set dance floors pounding from the 1930s until rock and roll arrived in the 1950s and dances moved to a different groove. The queues at the jazz box-office shortened after that, but the music was not declining – simply changing. Jazz musicians still wanted to discover truths in the heat of the moment with like-minded partners, and appreciative audiences still wanted to be there when it happened.

If you join that audience, you may find, as jazz listeners have for decades, that some people will raise an eyebrow at your choice. You might get told you're being deliberately perverse, for enjoying a maverick music that – compared to the classical repertoire, opera or pop – is for the most part only grudgingly supported by cultural establishments, the media or the entertainment industry. The improvisational spirit of jazz tends to make it the contrarian of contemporary music, and contrarians make at least as many enemies as friends. But the jazz effect since the music's birth early in the last century, has been to transform how we hear melody and rhythm, to inspire lasting changes in art, popular culture, dance and even speech, and to help free music-makers of all kinds, in all parts of the world, from the shackles of habit and received wisdom.

The objection that jazz is nowadays a golden-age music, no longer evolving and enjoyed only by sentimental older listeners, continues to be a widespread stereotype. But it's one that is easily despatched by a trip to almost any music college today, or to a gig by a young band or a concert-hall performance by a legendary figure in which older admirers and young converts rub shoulders.

Then there's the improvisation versus composition argument.

Some insist that improvisation is bound to produce music of less lasting worth. But J.S. Bach, Mozart, Lizst and many other colossi revered now only for their compositions were brilliant improvisers – differing only from jazz players in the materials they used. As artists in all fields know, there's no golden rule that work produced on impulse is inferior to that which ripens slowly, but that the creative process involves an interaction of the two.

Carefully composed long-form works are key parts of jazz history too, but Duke Ellington's or Charles Mingus's compositions would have been very different if the composition/improvisation tension (both artists often wrote music during rehearsals, drawing on their performers' interventions) had not been central to the process.

Jazz is now at least a century old, even if the 'J' word was not widely attached to the emerging music that invited it until around 1916. But once it had taken hold, it evolved with astonishing rapidity, squeezing and reshuffling the evolutionary changes of European music over many centuries into one. At first a predominantly African American folk art nurtured on streets and in brothels and dance halls in the early 20th century, it blossomed into an orchestral music of power and subtlety, and then became a mercurial chamber music of elegant symmetry and logic, as if Bach were at work in a Harlem dive. After World War II, jazz took on a cool and cerebral guise, a gospel-driven and blues-drenched one, a funky and hard-rocking one, a popular and expressive vocal and soul-powered one, and latterly a deviously rhythmic one with edgy hip-hop inflections. Today, jazz exists simultaneously in all these forms and is played by artists from very different cultures, all over the world – and its importance to the evolution of 20th- and early 21st-century music is perhaps now only being fully appreciated.

For the first time, jazz is widely recognised to have profoundly influenced much of the world's music, whether played in bars, folk clubs or on the street, or in concert halls and conservatoires. Pop styles, from rock, R&B, gospel, soul and funk, to rap and hip-hop have been touched by it, through slow mutation of African traditions of percussion and vocal music, in work songs, hymns, ragtime dances, the music of funeral and wedding-bands and the blues. Jazz rhythms and phrasing also had a dramatic impact on some of Western pop's earliest songwriters, and 20th-century classical artists too – including composers Igor Stravinsky, Maurice Ravel and Leonard Bernstein, and such instrumental stars as Sergei Rachmaninoff and Vladimir Horowitz, who were admirers of the jazz piano virtuoso Art Tatum. Jazz influenced dance choreographers such as Alvin Ailey and Bob Fosse (Ailey brought the inspiration of Duke Ellington and the tradition of the blues into his work), and the abstract painters Jackson Pollock and Willem de Kooning were jazz fans who applied fast and spontaneous improvisational methods to visual art. The fiction of F. Scott Fitzgerald, Toni Morrison, Milan Kundera and many other 20th-century writers also reflect the reflexive energies of jazz.

If we were to take an imaginary journey around the world in search of live jazz today, we might well be astounded by the diversity of it all. We might hear the Norwegian saxophonist Jan Garbarek blending the sounds of American free-form jazz with the traditional rural music of his homeland in the unlikely jazz setting of a great cathedral. Manchester clarinetist Arun Ghosh might be heard giving the modern-jazz form of bebop a Bangladeshi spin. We might hear a Japanese *avant-garde* percussionist and a French pianist joining wild free-improvisation and oriental chants in Paris – or Abdullah Ibrahim, the octogenarian composer and pianist mingling Zulu choral traditions, Christian hymn-harmonies, and the American jazz of Duke Ellington and Thelonious Monk in South Africa. The Pakistani Sachal Studios Orchestra from Lahore might be heard giving Dave Brubeck's famous hit 'Take Five' a new treatment, mingling Western and Eastern instruments and rhythms. If our jazz tour visited the American singer-songwriter Madeleine Peyroux, the influence of Billie Holiday would be plain, as the inimitably genial growl of Louis Armstrong would be in a performance by Tom Waits or Dr John. And speaking of Louis Armstrong...

'Jazz is only what you are,'

Armstrong himself said. Of course it's true of all artists, in all times and places. But, as the American critic Gary Giddins observed, 'it is most true of jazz, where eccentricity and idiosyncrasy are treasured'. This is the secret of a music that can keep you enthralled, fascinated and endlessly surprised for a lifetime.

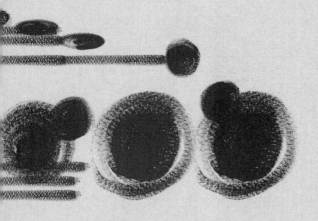

2 A HUNDRED YEARS OF JAZZ IN SIXTY MINUTES

Jazz burst out of the street parades, dancehalls, funeral marches and bordellos of old New Orleans, set the world dancing in the 1920s – and grew up fast from a rough-hewn folk art to a sophisticated orchestral music in its first 20 years.

When a boisterous quintet of young white musicians from New Orleans became the darlings of New York's chic set at Reisenweber's Cafe in February 1917, and had a bestselling single with 'Livery Stable Blues' and its flipside 'Dixie Jass Band One-Step', the world woke up to a new kind of music.

They called themselves The Original Dixieland Jass Band (ODJB), and to many of their new fans that brassy dance music might easily have erupted without a history, from nowhere.

But the ODJB and their New Orleans contemporaries would have known better. Long before this new music was ever called 'jass' and subsequently 'jazz', its sound had filled the streets and dancehalls of locations worlds away from the sophisticated East Coast. In southern cities from the early 1900s, marching band tunes, dance melodies and hymns had begun to be recast as collectively improvised, rhythmically dynamic conversations between cornet players, trombonists and clarinetists. Drummers were introducing a slyly syncopated kick on the off beats. The haunting, sliding-pitch intonation of the blues made these musicians' instrumental lines sound like voices.

But jazz went back further than that. The deepest roots of the story went back centuries.

OUT OF AFRICA

An African American music had been brewing throughout the vicious centuries in which Africans were being stolen from their homelands in millions and dragged in chains to the New World as slaves. The songs, rituals and dances of West Africans were sustained by the survivors and then pragmatically tolerated by slave-owners to sustain their captives' morale. In turn, the Africans assimilated to their surroundings as best they could, finding their own ways to sing Protestant hymns, fitting their notions of pitch into unfamiliar European eight-note diatonic scales and learning to play violins and guitars.

Even across such stark divides, dialogues grew. By the 19th century, a sound distinctly audible as African American was emerging wherever there had been a slave population. Work songs accompanied the slog of labourers in the cotton fields and on the railroads. Gospel singing reinvigorated traditional Christian church music. Rural folk-singers developed the intimate, defiant poetry of the blues. African rhythms put the wayward 'rag' into formal European dances.

New music also surfaced on minstrel shows, though these were forms of diversion originally conceived by whites for the mockery of African Americans. The spiritual or jubilee song – a soulful blend of European and African religious music – evolved on minstrel stages, and became a respectable concert hall attraction through the work of acclaimed ensembles such as the Fisk Jubilee Singers during the 1870s.

But what made all these fragments become a critical mass, from which jazz would erupt? The answer was proximity. By the start of the 20th century, musicians with very different experiences and techniques were beginning to rub shoulders in some key locations, mostly in the south.

In southern seaports such as Charleston and New Orleans, there was plenty of input from other immigrant cultures too – rural French brass band traditions and the French fiddle music that became zydeco, Celtic folk melodies, beer hall music sung by German draymen, the African-derived superimposition of two-beat over three-beat triple time that came to New Orleans in tangos and also as the Cuban *habanera*. Socially, the divisions between African American labourers and the better-off Creoles of mixed African and European birth receded in the later years of the 19th century, as new racist laws increasingly hit both groups.

A different audience for entertainers was emerging, excited by the promise of a new century and hungry for fresh sounds and dances.

New Orleans also kept African cultural traditions alive long after the slave trade had ended. In Congo Square, the authorities had allowed the slave population a weekly celebration of the traditions of the African homeland. Congregations of singers, dancers and drummers ran into hundreds, celebrating a music of community life, not entertainment – a music of social interaction, religious ceremony, domestic work and hunting.

NEW ORLEANS

All the pre-jazz strands thus entwined in New Orleans, and in 1897 Alderman Sidney Story, of the City Council, fortuitously added another when he authorised a 16-block red-light district for the legal regulation of prostitution. Soon dubbed 'Storyville', it became a tourist attraction, and a source of booming employment for pimps, brothel-keepers and professional musicians.

There were bands of working-class African Americans who knew popular songs and dance tunes by ear. There were mixed-race Creoles with a French musical education and often a dual skill as wind players and violinists. There were influential whites such as the drummer, bandleader and booking agent 'Papa Jack' Laine, who hired players from most of the city's ethnic groups for his Reliance brass bands. And there was ragtime. Originally pioneered by a handful of minstrel-show dancers and pianists, and popularised by Missouri composer Scott Joplin, ragtime shifted the emphasis onto the weak beats in a bar line instead of the expected strong ones – creating a bracing marriage of opposites between a rhythmically capricious melody line and its strict left-hand partner. From that simple device came the new ragtime dance craze that had such an impact in the early years of jazz.

THE FIRST KING OF JAZZ

By the time Storyville was licensed, the conditions for jazz in New Orleans were close to ideal, and a completely new music's pioneers came to life. One of the first, and most feted, was Charles Joseph 'Buddy' Bolden, an African American cornetist who seemed to possess much of the hedonistic magnetism of a modern rock star. From the late 1890s, Bolden's sheer volume, expressiveness and blues power were reputedly stunning to witness and his influence around Louisiana was immense. Bolden seems to have played a mutated ragtime with a strong blues feel rather than the more flexible and fluid pulse of the jazz to come, but he was a charismatic creative influence during his brief strut on the pre-jazz stage.

Creole pianist Ferdinand LaMothe, better known by his suggestive nickname of 'Jelly Roll' Morton, shared Bolden's fondness for fusing ragtime rhythms and the blues – and the more it was done, the more an excited public demanded it. Morton was a braggart. But if his claim that he invented jazz was exaggerated (though he did favour more fluidly jazzy four-beat rhythms over march-time's two-beat gait), he was nonetheless a creative musician to the core. Mixing ragtime and blues with classical and Spanish influences, he was to mature as a prolific composer, and as jazz music's first truly creative arranger too.

Morton was the most prominent of a forward-looking group of turn-of-the-century Creoles, including cornetist Freddie Keppard (whose Olympia Orchestra had by 1909 furnished the blueprint for the ODJB), the clarinet prodigy (and subsequently brilliant saxophonist) Sidney Bechet and trombonist Edward 'Kid' Ory, a natural bandleader and an even better talent spotter, who hired local cornetist Joe Oliver in 1914 for the latter's evocative blues sound, and colourful range of mute-produced sound effects that led Ory to market him as 'The King of the Cornet'. And when The King moved to Chicago amid the great northward labour migrations of working-class southerners in 1919, Ory smartly replaced him with a callow teenager from the tough New Orleans ghetto.

The newcomer's name was Louis Armstrong.

LOUIS ARMSTRONG

In the 1920s Armstrong was the dazzlingly original instrumentalist and occasional vocalist that almost everyone in music wanted to sound like, and if any single individual could be said to have hauled jazz from its homespun origins and turned it into a thrilling, subtle and many faceted modern art form, it was him. When a 20-year-old Armstrong joined King Oliver's new Creole Jazz Band on a residency at the Lincoln Gardens Café on Chicago's South Side in July 1922, the sound of the two cornetists fluently trading blues phrases represented a level of jazz playing way above the ODJB's jokey vaudevillian act.

Oliver played closer to the tunes, but varied his sound with tone changes and vocalised effects. Armstrong flew off at tangents, often doubling the tempo of the song while the rhythm section stayed put, hurtling through fast lines that still fitted the structures perfectly, pushing and pulling the rhythm by phrasing his statements at unequal lengths. Pianist Lil Hardin, blues-steeped clarinetist Johnny Dodds and his subtle sibling 'Baby' Dodds at the drums made the quintet sound free yet astonishingly integrated.

When the Creole Jazz Band recorded in 1923, fans and players all over the States came up to speed with the real state of the art.

THE HARLEM RENAISSANCE
AND THE NEW ORLEANS SWANSONG

Louis Armstrong's influence on jazz development in the 1920s was immense, but he was never at work in a vacuum. He transformed how jazz of all kinds could be made, but jazz also changed around him in ways he did not control.

New ideas were circulating faster – via radio, records and improving transport. Mainstream record labels, including Columbia, Okeh and Victor, reacted to the appeal of their jazz, blues and gospel output; some even launched 'race records' imprints marketed to African Americans, with catalogues featuring new jazz bands and also an operatically powerful group of female blues singers, including Mamie Smith and her protégée, 'Empress of the Blues' Bessie Smith.

Louis Armstrong often added his magic to these blues sessions, but his most spectacular achievements of the 1920s were to represent both the apogee and the swansong of the New Orleans sound. Between 1925 and 1929, with the studio bands known as the Hot Fives and Hot Sevens (featuring old associates such as Johnny Dodds and Kid Ory and later Earl Hines), Armstrong's three-octave range embraced such soaring, beautifully structured improvisations that the character of jazz was irrevocably shifted from a primarily collective sound to a soloistic music. Woody Allen's character in the 1979 film *Manhattan* opines that Armstrong's 'Potato Head Blues' is one of the things that makes life worth living. Only Jelly Roll Morton's famous Red Hot Peppers sessions in the same period rivalled Armstrong's for creative use of New Orleans ideas and lasting musical influence.

So jazz music blossomed from being an obscure southern folk art sprung on an unsuspecting world through one rough-and-ready record in 1917, to a maturing new music for an increasingly demanding audience. New York audiences wanted their hot music to have a touch of elegance. Composers sought common ground on which hot jazz and the refinements of society dance bands and even classical ensembles could meet. There was a *vogue* for symphonic jazz, powerfully advocated by arranger Ferde Grofé and a former Denver Symphony Orchestra musician, Paul Whiteman, merging New Orleans improv and the rich textures of a classical orchestra.

Whiteman, who was a millionaire by 1922, commissioned composer George Gershwin's 'Rhapsody In Blue' and hired the musically sublime but tragically short-lived white cornetist Bix Beiderbecke, an improviser with a cool tone quite different to the New Orleans players, and melodic ideas that were in a comparable class to Armstrong's.

Jazz bands were getting bigger, and as they grew, so did the need for tighter discipline, good arrangements and musical notation. Paul Whiteman offered one solution, but his grand designs hampered creative jazz improvisation. A shy, young African American called Fletcher Henderson found a better

Louis Armstrong pulled his solo line away from the underlying beat, but knew just when to snap it back in. Bandleader Fletcher Henderson's arranger Don Redman copied the effect for his brass and reeds sections, and often had them knocking phrases back and forth in a

'call and response'

manner too.

way – and crucially contributed to a new Jazz Age, when the big band swing of the 1930s became the biggest pop music phenomenon the world had ever seen, before the arrival of rock and roll.

Henderson, a jobbing pianist for a Harlem music publisher, formed an orchestra in 1922. Within two years, he had hired Louis Armstrong and the 19-year-old tenor saxophonist Coleman Hawkins, and discovered a gifted arranger called Don Redman. It wasn't long before Fletcher Henderson was widely agreed to be running the most exciting black big band in New York.

One of his admirers was Edward Kennedy 'Duke' Ellington, a young pianist from Washington who had come to New York in 1923. Ellington and his Washingtonians band aimed to copy Henderson's methods at first, and possessed their own New Orleans stylists in the trumpeter James 'Bubber' Miley (a mute-specialist in the Oliver manner) and, for a brief period in 1924, the fiery Sidney Bechet. But it was when the handsome and stylish young bandleader landed the job of writing music for the opulent music-theatre routines at Harlem's Cotton Club, that his own creativity took off. The club was owned by mobster Owney Madden, and featured black artists performing 'jungle' shows depicting a caricature of African culture for a rich white clientele.

The Cotton Club presented quite different challenges to firing up a jitterbugging dance floor with hot tunes, as

Fletcher Henderson was doing at the Roseland Ballroom. They drew Ellington and his musicians into a new sound-world of sumptuous textural effects, atmospheric harmonies, dramatic key-changes and multiple themes – the kinds of changes of pace and mood familiar to classical composers, but thus far unknown in jazz. Ellington arrived at the Cotton Club in 1927, and soon acquired a hit record with 'Creole Love Call', a national radio audience through live broadcasts from the club, and the nucleus of a line-up of unique soloists including saxophonists Johnny Hodges and Harry Carney, trombonist 'Tricky Sam' Nanton, and many others, powerful individuals that would be associated with him for the next three decades.

The Cotton Club jungle routines, as calculated entertainment for whites, only tangentially reflected that 1920s' blossoming of African American music, art and literature that came to be known as the 'Harlem Renaissance' – a development that reflected growing African American anger over inequality, and the determination of some black artists to move beyond being passive entertainers and create work reflecting their own experiences and roots. But Harlem's real nightlife buzzed all around the Cotton Club's luxurious premises, in speakeasies and illegal drinking joints and in the rent parties held in private apartments. Virtuoso pianists playing boogie-woogie and the ragtime-derived stride often performed at these functions, including the jazz

'Rent parties' were organised by residents to raise cash with musical entertainment. Rents in the largely African American Harlem district were inflated, despite incomes for blacks being lower.

and classical pianist James P. Johnson, and his most famous pupil, the brilliant and versatile Thomas 'Fats' Waller – who was to become in his short life one of America's best-loved all-round entertainers.

THE CRASH

The Roaring Twenties ended with the 1929 Wall Street Crash, and the aftermath dubbed the Great Depression made the previously popular blues songs in the race records catalogues sound like reminders of hardships people weren't in the mood to hear. Some fine musicians gave up jazz, or worked for whatever they could get. But by 1935, three ingredients were to change the music's fortunes – President Roosevelt's New Deal for economic recovery, network radio, and an ambitious clarinet prodigy from Chicago, called Benny Goodman. Goodman's band had an unusual four-sax approach to harmony and a very tight ensemble sound, but its success did not come overnight. In the summer of 1935, the band had embarked on a cross-country tour, to a generally lukewarm audience reaction. But when they reached the Palomar Ballroom in Los Angeles on 21 August, an extraordinary reverse occurred. They started the night with some polite commercial dance music, and the crowd looked as bored as they had at many other stopovers on the trip. Then they cut loose on Jelly Roll Morton's 'King Porter Stomp', one of the jazz arrangements Goodman had bought from a financially struggling Fletcher Henderson. The audience stopped their desultory dancing and crowded around the bandstand, cheering. As it turned out, a local disc jockey called Al Jarvis had been regularly playing the jazziest incarnations of Goodman's music on his show, building a young audience that expected hot jazz from the band, not sleek ballroom tunes. In the annals of American popular music, August 21 1935 came to be widely hailed as the night the Swing Era was born. Big-band jazz took off as the nation's dominant popular music (and soon the world's), and Benny Goodman was hailed as the 'King of Swing'.

IT DON'T MEAN A
THING IF IT AIN'T
GOT THAT SWING

'It don't mean a thing if it ain't got that swing,' said Duke Ellington. But the 1940s saw a turnaround in what swing could mean, when a handful of young Harlem experimenters developed the complex and fast-moving bebop style, and the world first heard the names Charlie Parker and Miles Davis.

The power and coordination of the big bands, the showmanship of their leaders, the character of their instrumental soloists and the glamour and skill of their singers seemed like the jazz parallel to President Roosevelt's New Deal message of hope after the despondency of The Great Depression.

Stylistically, swing in the 1930s had some clear identifying marks – line-ups tended to be bigger, double bassists took to playing the four-beat as a loping walk, drummers developed a lighter and more lissome touch, sustaining the pulse on the cymbals rather than the snare drum. Soloists strayed further from the tune and built improvisations on its chord pattern instead of the melody. It was a thrilling sound, and it found a huge following. The big ballrooms took to switching bands on revolving stages so that as the final blasting chords of one outfit receded, the first of the next one swung into view, and the frantically lindy-hopping dancers never had to miss a beat.

William 'Count' Basie's Kansas City band had a different sound to Benny Goodman's, but his popularity with swing fans and dancers became almost as great. It was more deeply infused with the blues, and often used short, exclamatory chords like sudden shouts (riffs) rather than melodic arrangements as

Swing was both a technique and a style. Its technical qualities centred on the four-beat pulse, the groove that had begun to supersede rag-based jazz in the late 1920s. Syncopation added the

'one-two-three-four, one-two-three-four'

like a sashaying walk, rather than the jaunty

'one-two, one-two'

strut of New Orleans music. But syncopation was always at work. Irregular melodies constantly tugged at the steady pulse beneath, creating the exciting illusion that the swing groove was impetuously surging forward, or languidly hanging back, as both the writing and the improvising stretched some notes of the melody here, shortened others there.

backing for soloists. Basie had a brilliant crop of individualists, including the poetically subtle saxophonist Lester Young, trumpeter Wilbur 'Buck' Clayton, and two fine blues singers in Helen Humes and the powerful 'Mr Five by Five', Jimmy Rushing. But the Basie sound was primarily down to its unique rhythm section – with the canny, understated leader at the piano, double bassist Walter Page (one of the most skilful of the early walking-bassline specialists) and the silkily propulsive Jo Jones at the drums.

Duke Ellington's and Count Basie's bands were the best of the Swing Era's African American ensembles, but the bands of Jimmie Lunceford and drummer Chick Webb were talented and popular too. Among the white bandleaders – in an era in which orchestra line-ups often divided along racial lines – Artie Shaw (a clarinetist of comparable skills to Goodman's) enjoyed huge popularity with the hit 'Begin the Beguine', Charlie Barnet's orchestra inventively covered Ellington and Basie material, and Tommy Dorsey's outfit had a Goodman-esque balance of smoothness and solo power. The big bands also nurtured a gifted crop of imaginative singers. Chick Webb had discovered a teenage Ella Fitzgerald, who was to become as vocally fast, flexible and inventive as an improvising saxophone player, and a subtle interpreter of good songs. But her most astonishing technical feats were accomplished with an enduring warmth and informality that made it all sound easy.

If Ella Fitzgerald and Louis Armstrong were to become the best-loved vocal stars to have risen through jazz, Fitzgerald's contemporary Billie Holiday was perhaps the most intimately affecting. Holiday was quiet and confiding, as if she were singing to every member of her audience individually. She seemed young and world-weary at the same time, and her relaxed dialogues with soloists – including Lester Young and the pianist Teddy Wilson – were as resourceful as any instrumentalist's. Tommy Dorsey's most famous recruit was his 1940 engagement of a young singer from Hoboken, New Jersey, with laid-back jazz timing and a cool crooner's voice, by the name of Frank Sinatra.

Big band swing did not sustain its pivotal role in the tumultuous decade to come, but the innovations of the Swing Era survived and evolved into the 1950s and '60s. A unique landmark was laid on 16 January 1938 when New York's temple of classical music and high culture – Carnegie Hall – hosted an all-star jazz concert led by Benny Goodman. This prestigious concert confirmed a new recognition, beyond the world of the dance halls and nightclubs and coterie of knowledgeable buffs, that jazz was a vital driving force in 20th-century art.

BEBOP

America had come to love big band swing, but the brashness of the style in its most commercial guises bored the younger musicians and some sought a music that was more challenging to play and to listen to. African American artists, as they had in the Harlem Renaissance years, were also continuing to study Africa's history and the story of slavery, as well as seeking the respect afforded to European originals of modern art from Stravinsky to Picasso. From a jazz perspective, that meant steering the music towards a more serious identity, and one that was not designed primarily for dancers.

From around 1940, a group of disaffected swing band musicians began meeting after the night's bread and butter work was over, often in a nightclub called Minton's Playhouse, on Harlem's 118th Street, New York. Plenty of the jazz aristocracy would hang out there too, including Ellington, Goodman and Billie Holiday – but prominent among the budding experimenters were Goodman's young electric-guitar celebrity Charlie Christian, a former stride player and church organist called Thelonious Monk, the popular Cabell 'Cab' Calloway band's rebellious trumpeter John Birks 'Dizzy' Gillespie, drummers Kenny Clarke and Max Roach and a shy, dishevelled, technically prodigious young saxophonist from Kansas City called Charlie Parker.

They were all different, and they had no sense that they were initiating a musical revolution. They were simply young and talented adventurers playing with new ideas. But the musically educated Gillespie's insights into chords and harmony, Christian's ability to veer apparently out of tempo without losing the music's groove, the diversity of Parker's improv ideas even at headlong speeds and over implausibly fast-changing chords, were all advances that unleashed the third jazz revolution within three decades. However, it was a revolution not always steered by its instigators. On 7 December 1941, Japan attacked America's Pearl Harbor naval base in Hawaii, and the United States entered World War II – so wartime economies and the enlistment of troops quickly hit the availability of fuel, shellac for record production and the big bands' substantial personnel. There was also a royalties dispute between the American Federation of Musicians and the record industry so there were no new recordings between August 1942 and November 1944. The ban's effect on bebop was that it was barely known outside of a handful of jazz clubs in its formative years. But the US government's cabaret tax, levied from 1944 on any establishment providing sustenance and music for dancers, had positive implications for the new music. If nobody danced, nobody was taxed, so promoting music intended only for listening was exempt. Bebop fitted the bill perfectly.

The most open-minded of the older generation got the point of bebop, and willingly hired its practitioners. Earl Hines

The name

bebop, or rebop,

came from the rhythmic nonsense syllables of wordless scat singing in imitation of saxophone and trumpet solos. The most musically advanced swing players, such as saxophonist Coleman Hawkins and the phenomenal blind pianist Art Tatum had already moved away from the basic improvising building blocks of three-note chords and 7ths, and could use the expanded melodic potential of the

'weird chords'

such as 11ths and 13ths, but bebop took the process much further, changing not just jazz harmony, but its melodies and rhythms too.

(Louis Armstrong's piano partner on the famous 'Weather Bird' duet in 1928) was one, as were Hines' singer Billy Eckstine and swing tenor saxophonist Coleman Hawkins, whose great 1939 recording of 'Body and Soul' had also been harmonically bop-like. In 1945, a quintet led by Parker and Gillespie introduced a clutch of new themes that came to be regarded as bebop anthems, such as 'Now's The Time', 'Groovin' High' and 'Ko-Ko'.

This was not simply technical tightrope walking for its own sake – bebop was never just a cerebral pursuit. The boppers were establishing an atmosphere of anticipation, freshness and excitement through this mercurial new music. But they were still deploying such familiar practices as theme and variation, tension and release, contrasts of reflectiveness and intensity – and often very explicit evocations of sadness and joy or love and loss, through the inflections of the blues – that mirrored the methods of musical artists of all kinds down the centuries.

The modernity of bebop, however, was inevitably a big part of its appeal in its first years. And some fans, looking for alternatives not just in music but in the meanings of life, turned the new style into a subculture – even a religion, with Charlie Parker as its messiah.

Charlie Parker was at his most productive in the latter half of the decade, but also at his most volatile. His narcotics addiction had led to a split with Gillespie and the formation of a new quintet with a 19-year-old trumpeter, Miles Davis.

These quintets recorded some of Parker's finest work, and he remained immensely productive until 1951, with his own bands, a classical strings ensemble, Afro-Cuban groups and on trips to Europe in 1949 and 1950. His health held out until 1953, and he died in March 1955, at the age of 34.

But if bebop dominated jazz in the 1940s and '50s, it also lived alongside mutations of big band swing, revivals of interest in early New Orleans music, and joined with imports from European formal techniques that shared as much with classical chamber music as jazz.

At the beginning of the 1940s Duke Ellington had formed the finest orchestra he had ever led, producing some of his most memorable music with the assistance of arranger Billy Strayhorn, with Ben Webster emerging as a new star soloist on tenor saxophone, and the young double bass virtuoso Jimmy Blanton – who played with the intricate vivacity of a bebopper – rekindling the rhythm section. Larger groups led by Stan Kenton, Woody Herman and Claude Thornhill all revealed an interest in European hybrids and explored longer pieces with more complex narratives than the slam-bang swing themes of the 1930s. Dizzy Gillespie briefly formed a typically extrovert big band to combine the influences of bebop, Afro-Cuban music and swing.

Kenton hired the Parker-influenced alto saxophonist Art Pepper, Herman had powerful swing drummer Dave Tough and a versatile and skilful sax section, and the band of Claude Thornhill – the least jazzily unfettered of them, but unintentionally an incubator of the coming Cool School – had a distinctive composer and saxophonist in Gerry Mulligan,

The classic early-bebop themes exhibited a stark beauty, headlong impatience and structural subtlety unlike anything heard in jazz before. The elasticity of the soloists' timing in relation to the underlying pulse (always a jazz fundamental) was now so audacious that the results could sound like missed cues, or endings arrived at too early – a practice the beboppers called

'turning the beat around.'

Chords also changed far more often in bebop than in swing tunes – offering constantly shifting melodic alternatives to the most skilled improvisers.

and a melodically devious alto saxophonist in Lee Konitz. But, crucially, Thornhill employed a brilliant self-taught arranger from Toronto, the Ellington-inspired Gil Evans. Evans' orchestral collaborations with Miles Davis from the 1940s to the '60s would go on to produce some of the most atmospheric and widely loved music in post-World War II jazz.

Whilst Thornhill, Evans and Mulligan would brood on visions for a new kind of jazz band. Miles Davis, a restrained player by nature, joined Mulligan's and Evans' speculations in the latter's New York apartment – and between them, they cooked up the game-changing 'Birth of the Cool' nine-piece band. It featured the soft glow of French horns and the keening sounds and whispers of oboes and flutes as well as conventional jazz instruments. It did not depend on modified Broadway songs for its material, and instead emphasised subtlety of texture and tone more than the intricacies of fast-moving improvisation.

While the tracks recorded at the Birth of the Cool sessions were commercial flops, they represented artistic breakthroughs that would lead to other visionary collaborations between Davis and Evans (notably the series of orchestral recordings that included 'Sketches of Spain' and 'Porgy and Bess'), and lastingly influence the way future large-scale jazz could sound.

THE COOL
SCHOOL, BRUBECK
AND BEYOND

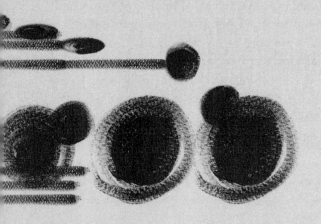

From the 1950s to the 21st century, jazz developed many identities – cool and restrained variations on bebop, rich orchestral tapestries, reprises of old swing styles, rootsy jazz fuelled by gospel, soul music and hip-hop, and refined forms close to modern classical music. Today, they all live side by side.

The Birth of the Cool band made a big impact on experimental jazz musicians, if not on the paying public. But some offshoots of the 'Cool' approach were more commercially successful. Gerry Mulligan led a popular quartet on the West Coast between 1952 and 1953 that concentrated on entwining lyrical melodies from two wind instruments – Mulligan and the Miles Davis-inspired trumpeter Chet Baker shared the front line. It was low-key, elegant and very tuneful and although much of the phrasing clearly linked to bebop, it didn't sound like a bop band.

A Californian pianist, Dave Brubeck, abandoned a veterinary course to study music with the classical composer Darius Milhaud, and did much to make fugues, rondos and other classical structures at home on the jazz stage. Brubeck's music was clever and intricate but it was catchy and song-like too. The combination of those qualities in a quartet that joined Paul Desmond (a discreetly soft-toned alto saxophonist), Eugene Wright (a bluesy African American double-bassist) and Joe Morello (a drummer of astonishing polyrhythmic flexibility) allowed the Brubeck quartet of 1959 to perform a very rare trick for modern jazz, in selling more than a million copies of the album 'Time Out', which included the iconic 5/4-time classic 'Take Five'. However, rivalling Brubeck's quartet for commercial appeal in this period was an African American ensemble that also used classical forms, but which creatively spliced the fastidiously delicate yet bluesy piano playing of John Lewis and the soulful and more boppish vibraphone sound of Milt Jackson. This was the Modern Jazz Quartet, usually named MJQ.

But the maverick of the entire Cool Jazz movement was the blind Chicago pianist Lennie Tristano – a scrupulous defender of an ascetic and anti-commercial kind of jazz. Tristano believed in the power of melody above all else. If improvisers could train themselves to play long solos of interesting melody lines without repetition or clichés, he reasoned, there would be no need for the usual audience-seducing moves, like repetitions of catchy familiar phrases or displays of technical bravura.

It was a purist approach, and awareness of Tristano's work is mostly restricted to jazz insiders now – but his influence through his most creative students was considerable. Dave Brubeck's saxophonist Paul Desmond, the composer of 'Take Five', was one. As was the classically graceful pianist Bill Evans (who some regarded as 'the Chopin of jazz piano'), the Birth of the Cool band's alto saxophonist Lee Konitz, and the dry-toned, melodically ingenious Los Angeles tenor saxophonist Warne Marsh. This understated and intricate kind of jazz-making was also reflected in the rise of the 1950s'

Third Stream movement (a term coined by composer and musicologist Gunther Schuller) to describe a music tending to deploy larger line-ups and more interplay with composers from modern classical music. But the most lastingly influential of all jazz borrowings from other disciplines surfaced in the work of a former jazz drummer turned composer, George Russell. He developed an idiosyncratically personal musical theory that turned into a book, *The Lydian Chromatic Concept of Tonal Organisation*. Finding new structural possibilities for jazz in sources as distant as mediaeval church scales, it offered improvisers a new toolkit based on cycles of modes instead of chords.

But if the older and more populist styles of jazz had been hit by tougher economics, changing tastes and the coming of rock and roll, they hadn't faded away. From the late 1940s and through the '50s, there was a powerful revival of interest in early New Orleans music – through the resurgence of the surviving pioneers, such as Willie 'Bunk' Johnson and Kid Ory, and enthusiastic adoption of the style by younger performers in the States and in Europe, including the UK's Humphrey Lyttelton, Chris Barber and Acker Bilk, and Claude Luter in France. Many of the great swing soloists of the 1930s, including Ben Webster, Coleman Hawkins, Roy Eldridge and Stan Getz, also retained enthusiastic followings, and the best of the big bands – Ellington's, Basie's, Woody Herman's and Stan Kenton's – continued to flourish.

Duke Ellington's return to popular recognition after the post-war big band slump was perhaps the most spectacular comeback of all. Having fallen out of favour, the Ellington orchestra played the Newport Jazz Festival in Rhode Island on 7 July 1956 – last on, after thunderstorms had dislodged much of the audience, they stunned the remaining listeners with a storming version of the leader's composition 'Diminuendo and Crescendo in Blue', on which tenor saxophonist Paul Gonsalves played 27 improvised choruses while handclaps, cheers and roars stirred him on and on. The event was a sensation.

Time magazine declared that the Ellington band 'was once again the most exciting thing in the business'.

BACK TO THE ROOTS
THE RISE OF HARD BOP

In the later 1950s, the eruption of rock and roll, with its African American roots in the blues and boogie-woogie mingled with white southern country music, was a catalyst to jazz developments of a more visceral vitality. So was the Civil Rights movement, with African Americans returning to the theme that new directions in a music identified with African Americans should draw more deeply on black American culture.

And so a counter reaction to the Cool School roared into life in the form of hard bop. It was simpler and more explicitly blues rooted than classic bebop.

Art Blakey, a bebop drummer who had played on early Thelonious Monk records, developed his Jazz Messengers band along these lines, and he often mixed a jazz-swing rhythmic feel with the strut of march time, as if he were in an old New Orleans street band. Pianist Horace Silver's music was some of the first jazz to be associated with that now ubiquitous word 'funk'. A group of rousingly holy-rolling Hammond organists that included Jimmy Smith and 'Brother' Jack McDuff, the soul-jazzy bands of the great R&B singer Ray Charles and the gospel bop outfits of saxophonist Julian 'Cannonball' Adderley were all popular exponents of this inclusive and communal style.

Hard bop used a lot of call-and-response phrase-swapping between soloist and band that emulated the church practice of preachers and worshippers exchanging exhortations and

stompingly rhythmic pieces

that encouraged congregation-like handclap accompaniment from the crowd.

Hard-boppers also liked long improvised solos, and the emergence of the 33rpm long-playing vinyl album finally enabled the heady atmosphere of live jazz shows to be fully represented on record.

A technically formidable New York tenor saxophonist, Walter 'Sonny' Rollins, the bands of former Parker drummer Max Roach, and a Miles Davis quintet that included a dazzling Rollins admirer, John Coltrane, were among the most prestigious of the younger groups that loosely fitted under the hard bop umbrella. In his strong gospel influences and willingness to mix rhythms from the whole of jazz history, the virtuoso double bassist Charles Mingus also fitted some hard bop criteria too. But Mingus was a gifted and independent creator with a profound interest in classical music as well as jazz. He was in another league to most of the hard bop bandleaders as a composer of longer works, and his stature in jazz history now puts him alongside Duke Ellington as one of the music's great original composers.

1959, FREE JAZZ AND THE PASSPORT TO THE WORLD

Though jazz was no longer defining the sound of popular music, it retained a loyal following through the 1950s and became increasingly diverse. Miles Davis's 'Kind of Blue', one of the best loved and bestselling of all jazz recordings, was a vaporous, slow-drifting jazz trance that was nonetheless full of subtly jazz-swinging rhythms and immensely moving improvisation. The music was based on a much simpler, cyclical rotation of modes along George Russell's lines, a simplicity that gave the music something of the timeless feel of an Indian raga.

Davis's saxophonist John Coltrane developed new blowing and fingering techniques to produce 'multiphonic' effects that allowed chords to be played on what had been built as a single-note instrument. By these means, and by the strenuous technique of circular breathing that allowed seamless lines to be played without pause, Coltrane's music took on a density that came to be dubbed 'sheets of sound'. In some ways, this impassioned clamour distantly echoed the free yet harmonious choral sound of the African-rooted singers back in Congo Square over a century before.

Dave Brubeck's popular 1959 album 'Time Out' – a project originally sparked by the composer's fascination with Turkish street musicians playing a folk song in 9/8 time – also included the Top 40 hit 'Take Five' and a variety of experiments with rhythm between stretches of relaxed jazz swing. For the even more adventurous, there was the music of Ornette Coleman, a self-taught saxophonist who had grown up in the 1930s and '40s in Fort Worth, Texas. But by his own idiosyncratic route, he developed an intensely human and voice-like saxophone sound. Coleman was steeped in the sound of the blues, but he didn't care if they fitted into 12 bars or 20. He also swung irresistibly, and his astonishing tonal palette offered him the sounds of laughter, delight, derision or desperation. He was often fired from Texas R&B bands for his cavalier attitude to structure and pitch, but in the late 1950s he found the kindred spirits he needed. In double bassist Charlie Haden, trumpeter Don Cherry and drummers Ed Blackwell and Billy Higgins he found partners sensitive enough to improvise with him without identifiable means of support. Coleman gave the process a name: 'harmolodics'. For him, it represented a constantly changing relationship of melody, harmony and rhythm that the participating players rebalanced as they went.

The rise of free-jazz split the jazz community, and Coleman was admired as an intuitive genius by some, rejected as a charlatan by others. But he proved the doubters wrong. His methods have been adopted by younger jazz musicians, he went on to write symphonies and collaborate with opera singers and North African drum choirs alike – and initiate a funkier electric-fusion approach with his Prime Time band in the 1970s that's been as influential as his acoustic music.

JAZZ IN THE MELTING POT

As in the 1920s and the '40s, African American musicians brought anger and defiance at their continuing social and political marginalisation into jazz. In 1960, Ornette Coleman put Jackson Pollock's abstract painting *White Light* (1954) on the cover of his album 'Free Jazz: A Collective Improvisation' as a declaration that experimental jazz musicians stood in the vanguard of all modern art. Archie Shepp, a saxophonist heavily influenced by Coltrane, brought civil rights issues into his work in jazz performances, polemical writings and appearances as an actor. Sonny Rollins recorded 'Freedom Suite' from similar motivations, drummer Max Roach made 'We Insist! Freedom Now Suite'. Pianist Cecil Taylor brought all these elements into such tumultuous fusion by virtue of such an astonishing keyboard technique that it was almost impossible for listeners to unpick which strand within his music had come from which source. Saxophonist Albert Ayler, who saw himself as a jazz missionary, took his vision for jazz all the way back to the incantations and wails of religious rituals, and to eerily dissonant variations on early marching music and R&B.

Meanwhile, the accessible hard bop and soul-jazz styles stayed popular, and a seductive descendant of Cool School music hit the pop charts when the Lester Young-inspired former Woody Herman musician Stan Getz and Brazilian vocalist Astrud Gilberto made the 1962 album 'Jazz Samba', and its hit single follow-up 'The Girl from Ipanema'.

An even bigger change now swept over jazz as an international musical language. Up to the 1960s, its enthusiasts outside of the United States had still largely followed the examples of American models – even Jean 'Django' Reinhardt, the Belgian Romany guitarist with an untutored sense of harmony as uncanny as Louis Armstrong's.

But now the rules of admission had changed. The free jazz Ornette Coleman had envisaged allowed the Louis Armstrong dictum 'jazz is only what you are' to extend to musicians everywhere. John Coltrane's sound enthralled a 14-year-old Jan Garbarek, listening to the radio in Norway. Garbarek emulated Coltrane's tone and the unfettered cry of Albert Ayler in his youth and developed a unique saxophone sound influenced by his own country's folk music and vocal traditions. In Britain, the virtuoso saxophonist John Surman began as

Jan Gararabek was the player American composer George Russell called 'the most uniquely talented jazz musician Europe has produced since Django Reinhardt'.

a Coltrane disciple and developed a personal approach inflected by English choral music and folk songs. German saxophonist and abstract painter Peter Brötzmann took Coltrane and free jazz into even wilder terrains. In 1960s' Poland, as the Cold War thawed, composer and pianist Krzysztof Komeda and the Miles Davis-inspired trumpeter Tomasz Stańko reworked the American Cool School and hard bop sounds with their own kind of wry melancholia. In South Africa, jazz musicians harassed and separated by the racist apartheid system found ways to perform, and even play across segregated lines, and international stars such as pianist Abdullah Ibrahim (formerly known as Dollar Brand), trumpeter Hugh Masekela, and the British-resident exiles including pianist Chris McGregor and saxophonist Dudu Pukwana were inspired by jazz freedoms to find their own. In Brazil, the multi-instrumentalist Hermeto Pascoal joined his country's traditional dance forms to the American jazz influences of Miles Davis and others.

FUSION

A new word entered the jazz lexicon – 'fusion', which embraced a variety of liaisons between jazz methods and the sounds of rock and funk. Moog synthesisers, bass guitars, the distortion effects of rock guitarists like Jimi Hendrix and splicings of rock and dance rhythms into jazz bands were allowing some versions of the music to return to the dance floor.

Miles Davis's saxophonist Wayne Shorter and pianist Joe Zawinul combined to form the dynamic, danceable and orchestrally-textured fusion band Weather Report in 1970 and ran it for 15 years. Davis began listening to black soul and R&B artists such as Sly Stone, but also to the modern classical composer Karlheinz Stockhausen, and started applying electronic technology to his trumpet sound that could make him resemble a keyboard, a guitar or a saxophone. But he still improvised freely, often more uninhibitedly than in his Cool Jazz days, and when he drifted into a soft love song, he still sounded like no other ballad player in the world.

Davis's young drummer Tony Williams even led a power trio called Lifetime that teamed him up with British guitarist John McLaughlin and bassist and singer Jack Bruce – a global music celebrity for his partnership with Eric Clapton and Ginger Baker in the thrilling rock trio Cream. Jazz had also found its way back to a big soul, R&B and pop audience in the work of crossover star George Benson – whose imaginative guitar lines

In the 1980s, mainstream jazz films were made, such as jazz fan Clint Eastwood's *Bird* (a biopic of Charlie Parker)and Bertrand Tavernier's *Round Midnight*.

had been heard on a raft of bluesy Hammond organ albums, but who reinvented himself in 1976 as a soul singer (albeit one whose guitar sound could still be traced back to Charlie Christian) with the hit song 'Breezin'. Herbie Hancock, a brilliant jazz pianist, had a parallel existence as a composer of dance hits, often applying studio production techniques used by DJs. But the enduring virtues of traditional acoustic music were asserted by, amongst others, pianist Keith Jarrett, a maestro equally fluent with the most taxing classical as well as jazz materials, who made an entirely improvised live solo piano album, 'Köln Concert' in 1975. It became the bestselling piano album in any idiom, and made Jarrett a major star.

The music began to be widely taught in colleges and schools, and in Britain an inspirational saxophonist from a Caribbean family – Courtney Pine – emerged from a reggae background to show his generation of young black Britons that this ostensibly mysterious and technically forbidding music could be for them, too. Pine coupled an advanced technique with the instincts of a popular entertainer.

Sonny Rollins, the hard-bop star of the 1950s and '60s, became a bigger star in his senior years. A big band of former Charles Mingus sidemen also formed to celebrate the jazz composer's legacy and the Mingus Big Band became, and remains, one of the most popular draws on the international circuit.

JAZZ TODAY

Time magazine put the New Orleans-born Wynton Marsalis on its cover in 1990, and headlined the story 'The New Jazz Age'. The music that had seemed to be fading from the popular taste for over a decade was on the way back. Marsalis's influence did launch what was sometimes decried in jazz circles as a backward-looking neo-classical movement, but he knew exactly where his own roots and the roots of jazz lay.

Marsalis is a superb trumpeter with ostensibly effortless access to fresh phrasing in the passing moment and a rounded, joyous tone. In his first decade as a major new jazz voice in the 1980s, his talents allowed him to release albums of classical trumpet music and jazz alternately, and he went on to devote himself to recreating the music of Ellington, Mingus, Monk and many other legends for contemporary audiences who would otherwise only ever hear it on record. From the mid-2000s on, Marsalis also began to turn his prestigious Jazz at Lincoln Center Orchestra into a vehicle for new world music fusions, collaborating with Pakistan's Sachal Studios Orchestra and musicians from Spain and Ghana.

Pakistan's Sachal Studios Orchestra was a jazz-loving film soundtrack band from Lahore that performed such unique jazz interpretations as 'Take Five' played on sitars and tablas.

Jazz became a hip term again. DJs began playing old hard bop vinyl albums to audiences of dancing clubbers. Art

Blakey, still driving updated editions of the Jazz Messengers into his seventies, would turn up at gigs and be astonished to find troupes of young breakdancers spinning new moves to his music. McCoy Tyner, John Coltrane's powerful pianist in the pioneering 1960s' Coltrane quartet, also came closer to a rhythmically inviting, melodically seductive and frequently Latin-driven jazz on rekindling his career after his famous employer's death.

Jan Garbarek made a record with a British classical vocal group, the Hilliard Ensemble, and they developed a fusion of early music plainsong and church chants and Coltrane-inspired saxophone variations that on its recorded debut sold over 1.5 million copies. An American piano trio, The Bad Plus, developed a radical but popular method that flung together bebop, funk, free improv, Stravinsky and almost unrecognisable covers of cult pop hits such as Nirvana's 'Smells Like Teen Spirit'. The long-running line-up of piano, double-bass and drums so long associated with the classical elegance of Bill Evans' trios, enjoyed a renaissance. Florida-born, Brad Mehldau's approach was contrapuntal and classical, and often fooled audiences into wondering whether they were hearing a reprofiled pop hit, or Bach. The Norwegian Tord Gustavsen developed a big following for a quietly tiptoeing music mixing hymns from his homeland's churches and restrained but audible American gospel grooves. Britain's Django Bates, one of the architects of the uncategorisable 1980s' big band Loose Tubes, took to playing Charlie Parker tributes in a trio in 2011, transforming Parker's original conceptions whilst maintaining their diamond-hard clarity and economy, illuminating the composer's genius anew.

In the first dozen years of the 21st century, a jazz listener could embrace an astonishing variety of music, and hear the unmistakable sounds and inflections of jazz in all of it. Popular vocalists such as the smoky-toned American Diana Krall and the UK's Frank Sinatra-inspired singer and songwriter Jamie Cullum can now fill venues such as the Royal Albert Hall with listeners who may know little about jazz history, and quite a few that know a lot. But, like Nat 'King' Cole in the 1940s, or George Benson 30 years later, both of them were skilful jazz instrumentalists before they were singers, and the sensitive awareness of how jazz is phrased and swung is an undercurrent to everything they play.

Closer to the contemporary streets, the jazz muse connected with hip-hop and rap, notably through inventive crossover artists such as pianist Robert Glasper – or the brilliant drummer Chris Dave, who might conceal an iconic jazz piece like Coltrane's 'Giant Steps' amid a shower of percussion sound from drum machines and his own intricate polyrhythms. Rhythm tends to predominate over older conceptions of melody and harmony in 21st-century jazz and young audiences are increasingly gravitating to the newest incarnations of the music because of it.

Robert Glasper was a pianist of Herbie Hancock origins who has collaborated with major figures of hip-hop and contemporary R&B.

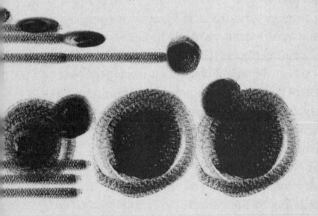

3

VISIONARIES –
THE FIRST WAVE

Signifying anything hot from all-round exuberance to sex, the slang word 'jass' was first hitched to the American Southlands' raucous new music in 1915. Soon the Jazz Age was sweeping the Western world, and a young man called Louis Armstrong blew his way out of a New Orleans ghetto to lead a 20th-century musical revolution.

THE FIRST WAVE

BUDDY BOLDEN (1877–1931)

The musician best suited to mythical stature in the first wave of jazz was the cornetist Charles Joseph 'Buddy' Bolden, because he died young, left no recordings and was committed to the Louisiana State Insane Asylum in 1907, aged just 30. He died there in 1931, and was buried in an unmarked pauper's grave.

Bolden's band played ragtime, blues and popular dance tunes, but his blowing power was thrilling, his blues sound moving, and he reputedly applied the syncopated 'Big Four' rhythmic skip to the steady gait of a marching band rhythm that freed up new spaces for improvising musicians.

Many New Orleans jazz pioneers recalled hearing Buddy Bolden, including Bunk Johnson, Freddie Keppard and Sidney Bechet – and a fascinated child called Louis Armstrong, who would remember the blazing sound of that cornet player who 'blew so loud'.

Buddy Bolden embellished ragtime, blues and popular dance tunes in his own ways. Imagine a drum and cymbal playing something bouncy and regular such as

'Boom-chi/boom-chi/boom-chi/boom-chi.'

Then hum a tune over the top, and the tune will tend to follow that steady pulse. But if the drum beat changes to

'Boom-chi/boom-chi/boom-chi/badoom-BOM'

with the drum and cymbal hit together on the final emphasis, the rhythm of the song has immediately changed to something more stretchy and flexible. It's an invitation for improvisers to create their own sound.

'JELLY ROLL' MORTON *(1890–1941)*

The Creole pianist and composer Ferdinand Joseph LaMothe, better known as 'Jelly Roll' Morton, didn't wait for others to suggest he didn't wait for others to suggest he invented jazz, he insisted on it himself.

Morton was a superb piano player and a relentless self-publicist. He wrote the first successful piece of jazz sheet music 'Jelly Roll Blues' in 1915, recorded exceptional piano solos, and with his Red Hot Peppers groups expanded the palette of a traditional New Orleans jazz band, varying pace and texture with a blend of solo and ensemble energy that laid some of the foundations for orchestral jazz.

Aged 14, 'Jelly Roll' Morton had been thrown out of home by his God-fearing aunt when she found out he was playing piano in a brothel. This led him to hit the road as an itinerant pianist.

Morton's career did not survive into the Swing Era of the 1930s, but recordings made with the ethnomusicologist Alan Lomax and preserved by the Library of Congress represent a unique document of reminiscences and performances by a gifted artist who was there at the very beginning. But in 1938 he was stabbed in a club, received poor medical care, and his attempts to rebuild his career thereafter were hampered by chronic ill-health until his death in Los Angeles in 1941.

SIDNEY BECHET *(1897–1959)*

Sidney Joseph Bechet was a Creole clarinetist and later soprano saxophonist whose improvising genius was as formidable as Louis Armstrong's. As a child, he practised the fife, grew bored, and then borrowed his brother's clarinet and emerged as a prodigy on it. He heard Enrico Caruso on some of the first-ever gramophone records, and the opera singer's sound may have been the source of his famously broad vibrato on the soprano saxophone.

Bechet's method was similar to that of his pre-jazz peers – what was described at the time as 'variating' the main song's key melody – but he did it with a blistering conviction and attack that made the song completely his own. He joined New Orleans' prestigious New Olympia Band in 1914, toured with composer James Reese Europe's African American classical orchestra, working briefly with Duke Ellington (who called him 'the epitome of jazz') and wound up a folk hero in his adopted France after World War II with a chart hit record 'Petite Fleur' and a statue in Juans-les-Pins to prove it.

JOE 'KING' OLIVER *(1881–1938)*

Louisiana-born Joseph Nathan Oliver, known as Joe Oliver, and later King Oliver, was a respected figure for his powerful sound and colourful range of mute-generated sound effects (even using sink plungers, hats or bottles covering the bell of the cornet).

He played trombone and cornet as a regular member of marching bands, and joined Kid Ory's popular ragtime-driven band before his move to Chicago in 1918.

Oliver's accomplished Chicago outfit included the most creative female instrumentalist in early jazz (pianist Lillian Hardin, later Louis Armstrong's wife), and in 1922 he created one of the most significant of all jazz landmarks when he invited Louis Armstrong to be his front-line foil in the Creole Jazz Band. Every would-be jazz player within range came to hear that band – including clarinetist Benny Goodman and cornetist Bix Beiderbecke – and witness Armstrong's emergence from his chrysalis to become one of jazz music's greatest creators.

KID ORY (1886–1973)

Edward 'Kid' Ory was a banjoist first, then one of the most influential trombonists of the first phase of jazz. He developed the 'tailgate' trombone style, a strongly rhythmic approach that also used extensive melodic counterpoint and long, slurred notes. The name was probably derived from the trombonists' usual position on the promotional carts carrying New Orleans musicians around town – the tailgate being the only place with room for the instrument's lengthy slide. The story goes that Buddy Bolden discovered Ory at his home on Jackson Avenue

Joe 'King' Oliver's evocatively vocalised

'wah-wah'

effects were legendary, especially his three choruses on 'Dippermouth Blues'. He was a true polyphonic player, considering the group as a single instrument, knowing just when to embroider, observe or get out of the way of his partners' contribuitions.

in New Orleans, but the promising recruit was deemed too young by his family to share Bolden's unruly nightlife.

Kid Ory's band was the first African American jazz band to record when it went into the Nordskog studios on the West Coast in 1921. When a revival of interest in early New Orleans music and trad jazz occurred in the 1940s, a still-vigorous Ory was a key figure.

LOUIS ARMSTRONG *(1901–1971)*

A child of the New Orleans ghetto nicknamed 'Back o' Town' or 'the Battlefield', Louis Daniel Armstrong dropped out of school at 11, then sang in a street-corner barbershop quartet in which he learned to harmonise by ear and to sing 'scat' with nonsense syllables too. He learned the cornet in a reform school following his arrest for firing a gun in the street on New Year's Eve, 1912.

The teenage Armstrong was mentored by local cornetist Joe 'King' Oliver, learned to read music in Fate Marable's Mississippi steamboat band and then one of the best New Orleans ragtime-to-jazz bands led

Louis Armstrong was affectionately known as 'Satchmo' or 'Pops'.

by Kid Ory. In 1922, Armstrong answered Joe Oliver's call to join his Creole Jazz Band at Chicago's Lincoln Gardens Café, to form the two-cornet front line that launched one of the most expressive jazz relationships of the music's early years.

Armstrong seemed to combine all the skills of New Orleans' early jazz musicians in one player. He had the blowing power of a street-band performer, but extended to a dizzying upper range. He had a composer's sense of melodic shape as an improviser, drew listeners in with sly insinuations and playful twists, while his unerring rhythmic sense allowed him to stray audaciously off the beat. Armstrong's 89 tracks cut between 1925 and 1929 (the Hot Fives and Hot Sevens recordings) came to be regarded as the first unqualified masterpieces of the Jazz Age, and he accompanied the greatest blues singers of the era, including Alberta Hunter and Bessie Smith. In the 1930s, Armstrong became an idiosyncratically expressive vocalist as well as a trumpet virtuoso. He continued to record with his 1947 All Stars group into the 1950s, and became a much-loved mainstream star with the hit vocals 'Hello, Dolly' and 'What a Wonderful World'.

BIX BEIDERBECKE (1903–1931)

Leon 'Bix' Beiderbecke grew up in middle-class Iowa, a long way from the tough streets of New Orleans' ghetto. But the self-taught cornetist and pianist (whose unorthodox technique and interest in modern classical music gave him a pure, bell-like sound quite different from the brash brass sounds of the period) was rooted in the New Orleans approach, even if his own interpretation of it was distinctively cooler. Alcoholism killed Beiderbecke at only 28. But a peak of creativity that had bloomed for barely six years was enough for him to win the reverence of peers including Louis Armstrong, for uniquely introspective solos that relied on his burnished tone, patient note-selection and pacing rather than bravura extremes. For these, and for piano compositions influenced both by jazz and the impressionism of Claude Debussy and Maurice Ravel, the eminent musicologist Gunther Schuller was later to describe Beiderbecke as 'the greatest white jazz musician of the '20s'.

The youngest of three children raised in a prosperous household in Davenport, Iowa, the boy was picking out piano melodies by ear from early childhood. He heard jazz bands on the passing riverboats, and when as a teenager he heard Nick LaRocca's cornet playing with the Original Dixieland Jazz Band on his brother's phonograph, he taught himself LaRocca's melodies. At boarding school in Illinois, Beiderbecke often played hooky to hear jazz in nearby Chicago, joined the Wolverines band in 1924, then worked with groups led by pianist Jean Goldkette and saxophonist Frankie Trumbauer, the latter a like-minded player of subtly understated music. In 1927, Beiderbecke and Trumbauer joined Paul Whiteman's hitmaking 'symphonic jazz' orchestra, but the former's drinking made him an unreliable employee. Beiderbecke was fitfully freelancing in New York with bandleaders including the Dorsey brothers and Benny Goodman at the time of his death.

ORIGINAL DIXIELAND JAZZ BAND (ODJB)

Like many ensembles formed to satisfy a market-led demand, the ODJB came together because a promoter wanted to bring a hot Dixieland combo to Chicago's Schiller's Café. The all-white line-up fluctuated, but eventually a contingent made the gig in March 1916 – Alcide Nunez on clarinet, Nick LaRocca on cornet, Eddie Edwards on trombone, Henry Ragas on piano and Johnny Stein on drums. Stein was dropped and Tony Sbarbaro came up from New Orleans. In 1917 they played a successful run at Reisenweber's Café in New York, and the first ever jazz recording was made by them shortly afterwards. The ODJB's 'Livery Stable Blues' and 'Dixie Jass Band One-Step' were issued on 7 March – tracks that mixed elements of African American jazz methods, and a jokey showbiz approach drawn from minstrelsy and vaudeville. The release was a bestseller, turning jazz into a national craze. The ODJB came to England for a long residency at the newly opened Hammersmith Palais in 1919, triggering considerable interest in jazz among European musicians, and playing for the British royal family. Returning to the States in 1920, the band kept working, but its success was outstripped by the popularity of symphonic jazz and swing.

THE BIGGER PICTURE
OTHER KEY CONTRIBUTORS TO EARLY JAZZ

Willie Gary 'Bunk' Johnson (1889–1949) was a popular early New Orleans cornetist with a warm and relaxed sound, who later became a revered figure of 1940s' 'trad' revivalism. Cornetist Freddie Keppard (1890–1933) was a Creole with a ragtime-driven manner of phrasing, and his success as a bandleader led him to pioneer touring the early New Orleans sound to other parts of the USA. Keppard's favoured instrumentation (cornet, clarinet, trombone, piano and drums) was the model for the Original Dixieland Jazz Band.

King Oliver's 1922 Creole Jazz Band with Louis Armstrong included the most creative female instrumentalist of the era in pianist Lillian 'Lil' Hardin (1898–1971). Clarinets provided important stitching in the collectively played tapestries of the early bands, and notable exponents included Jimmie Noone (1895–1944) – a rich-toned player who had studied with Bechet – and Johnny Dodds (1892–1940), a staple member of the Creole Jazz Band and Armstrong's Hot Fives and Sevens, who had a haunting vibrato and a moving blues sound. And though the bands of Buddy Bolden, King Oliver or Jelly Roll Morton dominated first-generation New Orleans jazz, the society dance band of violinist and drummer John Robichaux (1866–1939) was influential, as was the Olympia Orchestra led by violinist A.J. Piron (1888–1943).

The cultural and musical diversity of New Orleans made it the hub of early jazz, but aspects of the music's character were forming elsewhere. Memphis-based composer W.C. Handy (1873–1958) had a big commercial hit with his 1914 composition 'St Louis Blues', a success that drew jazz and the blues ever more closely together. In New York, composer James Reese Europe (1881–1919) brought an African American symphonic music influenced by ragtime to Carnegie Hall and into the consciousness of white America – almost a decade before The Jazz Age had begun.

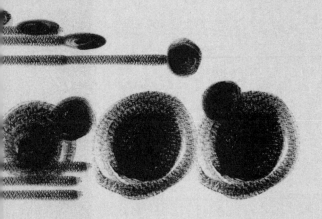

4 VISIONARIES –
THE SWING ERA

The seeds of the swing or big-band era were planted in the early 1920s, but the style boomed in the following decade. It represented a synthesis of New Orleans and symphonic jazz methods, and big-band jazz was the Western world's pop music up until World War II. Some key bandleaders and soloists helped shape this musical revolution.

BANDLEADERS

FLETCHER HENDERSON (1897–1952)

In 1924, James Fletcher Hamilton Henderson, Jr was considered by many to lead the best African American big-band in New York. Fletcher Henderson had gone north from Georgia as a shy 22-year-old with piano skills and a chemistry degree – but though there wasn't much work for black chemists in 1920s New York, his piano skills found him work with a Harlem music publisher, and soon as a dance-band leader influenced by both New Orleans jazz, and the smoother symphonic methods of Paul Whiteman and his arranger Ferde Grofé. By 1924, he was big enough to play New York's famous Roseland Ballroom, with Louis Armstrong as his star recruit.

The effect was spectacular. Armstrong's phrasing and timing inspired not just Henderson's other soloists (including the founding father of jazz tenor saxophone, Coleman Hawkins) but also the writing of Don Redman, an arranger already versed in symphonic jazz. But Henderson didn't keep up with changes in jazz in the 1930s, and struggled in the Depression. He sold his best arrangements to rival bandleader Benny Goodman, faded from the limelight and died in New York in 1952. His role had been briefly pivotal, however.

DUKE ELLINGTON (1899–1974)

The most famous name in all orchestral jazz, pianist, bandleader and composer Edward Kennedy 'Duke' Ellington got his nickname for his courtly manner and sharp clothes.

Ellington came to New York from Washington in 1923. Hired to compose for the Cotton Club's cabaret and music-theatre shows, he learned how to shape a sophisticated jazz band for an assignment quite different to simply playing for dancers. With the help of African American classical composer Will Vodery and fiery soloists that included saxophonist Sidney Bechet and cornetist James 'Bubber' Miley, Ellington met the Cotton Club challenge with early classics such as 'The Mooche', and went on to write many concerto-like compositions in partnerships with band-members, with arranger Billy Strayhorn crucially assisting after 1938. Ellington toured until his death in 1974, often playing the large-scale sacred music of his later years in churches and cathedrals.

Duke Ellington wrote around 2,000 compositions, often while on the road, from songs to suites, film scores and religious works.

COUNT BASIE (1904–1984)

If Duke Ellington wove symphonic tapestries around the unique sounds of particular soloists, William James 'Count' Basie was the Swing Era's master of rhythm. Using a light percussion sound, a steadily-walking double-bass groove, a punchy ensemble sound behind soloists using emphatically accented riffs, and his own cannily minimal piano style, Basie created a uniquely light and danceable sound. He came from Red Bank, New Jersey, played the ragtime-like stride piano style in vaudeville, and formed his own band in 1935 out of the remains of the late Bennie Moten's Kansas City Orchestra with saxophonist Lester Young, drummer Jo Jones and blues singer Jimmy Rushing. Basie's band became one of the most popular of the 1930s. It receded after World War II, but came back, recording the acclaimed 'The Atomic Mr Basie' album in 1957. After Basie's death in 1984, the ensemble continued to perform its best-loved pieces under the leadership of various band members.

BENNY GOODMAN (1909–1986)

Benjamin David 'Benny' Goodman was one of 12 children from a family of Russian-Jewish immigrants, raised in poverty in Chicago in the 1910s and 1920s. He studied classical clarinet but loved African American jazz, and by 14 was the family breadwinner as a musician. Goodman's perfectionism and discipline helped the band he formed in 1934 to sound tighter than most of the period's orchestras. His 1935 gig at the Los Angeles Palomar Ballroom was ecstatically received by a young audience, and is often cited as the real beginning of the Swing Era. Goodman featured star soloists (a racially-mixed line up, which was rare for the time) that included the pioneering guitarist Charlie Christian, vibraphonist Lionel Hampton and drummer Gene Krupa. His famous 1938 concert at Carnegie Hall helped raise the profile of jazz as an art. Goodman played classical music as well as jazz, and regularly toured worldwide from the 1950s to the '70s.

SOLOISTS

BESSIE SMITH *(1894–1937)*

The swing saxophonist Bud Freeman described the huge sound and emotional subtlety of Tennessee-born singer Bessie Smith as 'making something religious out of a popular song.' Smith's roots were in the blues, and her natural habitat was the travelling vaudeville circuit and the theatre rather than dance-halls or nightclubs – but if she was not exclusively a jazz or swing singer, she was nonetheless one of the most respected, affecting and popular African American vocalists of the 1920s and '30s. Singing for a living by the age of 15, she worked for a year in the travelling vaudeville company of

Gertrude 'Ma' Rainey – but her precocious emotional maturity, blues feeling, and intelligent handling of lyrics made her a leader by the early 1920s.

Though deservingly dubbed 'the Empress of the Blues', Smith was an untypically versatile kind of blues artist, able to improvise dialogues with some of the best jazz musicians of her era (including Louis Armstrong, Fletcher Henderson and stride piano star James P. Johnson), growl and bend notes with the expressiveness of King Oliver's cornet, and bring fresh interpretations to popular songs from vaudeville and musicals. Smith's 1923 recording debut with 'Downhearted Blues' brought her overnight fame, she appeared in the film *St Louis Blues* in 1929, and sensationally recorded the Depression lament 'Nobody knows you when you're down and out' the same year, but the popularity of the blues form and the stability of Smith's personal life both slipped downhill during the 1930s. She died following a road crash in Clarksdale, Mississippi in 1936. Smith's power to make almost any kind of song her own not only influenced subsequent jazz, blues and soul singers (notably Billie Holiday in her early years), but the voice-like intonations of jazz instrumentalists too.

COLEMAN HAWKINS *(1904–1969)*

Coleman Randolph Hawkins was one of the first to rescue the tenor saxophone's sound from a jokey farmyard-noise effect in vaudeville shows and turn it into a jazz voice of authority and eloquence. Hawkins was taught piano, cello and then saxophone in childhood, and worked with blues singer Mamie Smith's Jazz Hounds when he was 17. He then joined Fletcher Henderson in 1924 and built a worldwide reputation for his power, rich tone and melodic resourcefulness. He played in Paris with guitarist Django Reinhardt in 1937, as part of a long trip to Europe, before returning to the US in July 1939 to record a solo on 'Body and Soul' that was a masterpiece of variation on a song's chords. In the 1940s he worked with the leading beboppers, and toured with his own groups and with impresario Norman Granz's 'Jazz at the Philharmonic' all-star packages in the 1950s and '60s.

LESTER YOUNG *(1909–1959)*

Alongside Coleman Hawkins, the other founding figure of the tenor saxophone was Lester Willis Young – a brilliant melodist, whose tonal delicacy gave him a uniquely whimsical, cajoling sound. Young played in his father's family band, toured the Mid-west with Walter Page's Blue Devils in 1930, and famously outplayed Hawkins and other leading saxophonists in an all-night jam session in Kansas City in 1933. In 1936, Young became a key soloist in Count Basie's band, and a widely copied

Lester Young studied violin, trumpet and drums before emerging as one of the great jazz saxophonists.

model for saxophonists, including the young Charlie Parker, who analysed his solos closely. Young also embarked on a series of hauntingly intimate musical dialogues with vocalist Billie Holiday, but his 1944 draft into the army severely affected his mental and physical health, and his work became more inconsistent in the 1950s, though he often performed to his old standards in a variety of groups with swing and bebop partners.

ELLA FITZGERALD *(1917–1996)*

She won the *Down Beat* jazz magazine's 'Best Female Vocalist' award for 18 years and 14 Grammy awards – yet Ella Jane Fitzgerald always retained a quality of spontaneous innocence, as if she were singing for friends at home. Her range was wide, her pitching flawless, and her wordless scat improvisations were as inventive as those of the best instrumentalists. Ella Fitzgerald was spotted as a 16-year-old amateur at Harlem's Apollo Theater, joined drummer Chick Webb's swing band in 1935, and had a popular hit with 'A-Tisket A-Tasket' in 1938. She briefly led Webb's band after his death in 1939, and became a much-loved solo star from the 1940s to the '90s. Fitzgerald's 'Song Books' series, dedicated to the greatest achievements of American popular songwriters, remains her most lasting, varied and evocative work.

BILLIE HOLIDAY *(1915–1959)*

Billie Holiday's imagination and quiet emotional power made her a unique jazz singer. Born Eleanora Fagan, she was put in care at ten after being sexually abused by a neighbour, and imprisoned with her mother for prostitution at 14, but she was soon singing in Harlem clubs. Her voice was both youthful and knowing, she strayed provocatively and sensually behind the beat, and advances in microphone technology allowed her to make a dramatic impact at low volumes. A sensational appearance at the Apollo Theatre in 1934 launched her career, and Holiday's late 1930s' work with pianist Teddy Wilson and saxophonist Lester Young influenced instrumentalists and singers throughout jazz. She performed with Count Basie and Artie Shaw in 1937–8 and in 1939 appeared at Café Society, a racially integrated nightclub in Greenwich Village. Club-owner Barney Josephson persuaded her to record 'Strange Fruit', a harrowing chronicle of racist lynchings, and with it she found a new audience beyond jazz circles. Problems with narcotics hampered her later career, though she was still capable of sublime performances. Holiday died from cirrhosis of the liver at the Metropolitan Hospital in New York in 1959, facing a narcotics possession charge on her deathbed. Her unique voice has been influencing singers within and beyond jazz ever since.

THE BIGGER PICTURE
OTHER KEY CONTRIBUTORS TO SWING

Pianist Earl Kenneth Hines (1903–1983), widely known as Earl 'Fatha' Hines, based his phrasing on New Orleans wind players, and freed himself from the repetitive left-hand rhythms of the stride piano style. 'Weather Bird', his 1928 duet with Louis Armstrong, is one of the great jazz performances. Hines also led exciting big bands and encouraged the young beboppers in the 1940s.

The first great European jazz musician emerged in the Swing Era. A caravan fire deprived Belgian Romany guitarist Jean 'Django' Reinhardt (1910–1953) of two left-hand fingers but he was still technically astonishing, a natural improviser who could soar away from a song's structural bonds and whose rhythm – playing drove groups like a drummer. Reinhardt's Quintette du Hot Club de France (with violinist Stéphane Grappelli) was one of the most acclaimed of all 1930s' European jazz groups. He performed with Duke Ellington's orchestra in 1946, and worked regularly in France until his sudden death from a brain haemorrhage in 1953.

Jean 'Django' Reinhardt's delicate compositions 'Nuages' and 'Stardust' are among his most enduring achievements.

The African American pianists Arthur 'Art' Tatum, Jr (1909–

1956) and Thomas Wright 'Fats' Waller (1904–1943) are the all-time giants of jazz piano who blossomed in the 1930s. Tatum, though almost totally blind, was a juggler of constant key changes and improvised left-hand/right-hand dialogues so dazzling that classical piano stars including Vladimir Horowitz and Sergei Rachmaninoff, came to hear him play. Tatum's 1950s' sessions for Norman Granz's Pablo label were among his most remarkable achievements.

Fats Waller (1904–1943), originally a stride pianist and an organist accompanying his baptist preacher father, became an early pop star and all-round entertainer, a phenomenal pianist, and a prodigious composer – songs like 'Ain't Misbehavin'', 'Honeysuckle Rose' and 'Handful of Keys' are jazz classics. Waller was also the first notable jazz organist.

Some contributors to swing were less conspicuous figures – like Will Vodery (1885–1951), the African American composer, arranger and conductor whose arrangements did much to ignite the success of the famous 1927 musical *Show Boat*. Vodery was not a jazz artist, but (whilst working with Duke Ellington on the 1929 musical *Show Girl*) he introduced the bandleader to an appreciation of classical composers Claude Debussy, Frederick Delius and Maurice Ravel that transformed Ellington's understanding of harmony.

The swing bands glittered with remarkable solo talents. The sound of tenor saxophonist Benjamin Francis 'Ben' Webster (1909–1973) mixed the gruff and cantankerous with the caressingly romantic, and it made him a cornerstone of Duke Ellington's exceptional 1940s' bands, on triumphs like 'Cotton Tail' and 'Main Stem'. Count Basie's trumpeter Buck Clayton was a fluent improviser with a polished sound, and Basie saxophonist Don Byas bridged swing and bebop approaches. Benny Goodman's guitarist Charlie Christian and vibraphonist Lionel Hampton pioneered new techniques on their instruments, and Goodman pianist Teddy Wilson was a Hines and Tatum disciple with his own refined style. The virtuoso trumpeter Roy Eldridge provided the foundations for bebop star Dizzy Gillespie's technique, and the short-lived Paul Whiteman, Benny Goodman and Tommy Dorsey trumpeter Bunny Berigan was a thrilling bravura player with a big sound and fertile imagination.

Swing offered both ingenious jazz and accessible entertainment, and delivery of the latter was often in the hands of singers – with just about every big band featuring at least one, and very often a male-female double-act. Some of the Swing Era's early vocal stars were making the transition from blues and spirituals to the popular songs of swing, as Mildred Bailey and trombonist Jack Teagarden did. Forceful blues singers including Jimmy Rushing, Joe Turner and Jimmy Witherspoon often fronted swing bands (particularly Kansas City ones), Cab Calloway and Billy Eckstine were more urbane and elegant performers, Eddie Jefferson pioneered the technique of vocalese (in which lyrics are set to the melodies of famous instrumental solos), and Anita O'Day, Dinah Washington, Sarah Vaughan, Carmen McRae and Mel Tormé were all gifted singers who could shift easily between swing and the new bebop. The bands of Chick Webb, Jay McShann, Charlie Barnet, Jimmie Lunceford, Artie Shaw and the Dorsey brothers were also widely popular and distinctive bearers of the 1930s' big band torch.

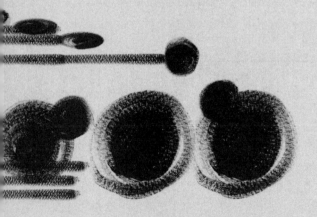

5

VISIONARIES – BEBOP AND POST-SWING

Spawned in the early 1940s by adventurous young experimenters in an after-hours Harlem club, the bebop style revolutionised the melodies, grooves and harmonies of jazz. By the late-'40s, its trailblazers – including Charlie Parker, Dizzy Gillespie and Thelonious Monk – were being hailed as giants of modern music.

THE BEBOP VANGUARD

CHARLIE CHRISTIAN (1916–1942)

Charles Henry 'Charlie' Christian became the first superstar of the electric guitar in 1939. Christian had learned guitar from his father on homemade instruments as a child. His jazz reputation spread around the Mid-west in his teens, and the pianist Mary Lou Williams recommended him to the producer John Hammond, which led to him being hired by Benny Goodman in 1939. When Goodman was ill and off the road in 1940–1, Christian passed the downtime at Minton's Playhouse, developing unprecedented variations on swing methods with Thelonious Monk, Kenny Clarke and others. Christian's inspirations were more often wind players than guitarists – he used supple single-line melodies far more than chords, extensively played chromatically (in half-tone intervals) and he began and ended phrases at intriguingly odd angles to the beat.

Christian's dynamic influence was cut short by his early death from tuberculosis in 1942, at the age of 25.

KENNY CLARKE *(1914–1985)*

Kenneth 'Kenny' Spearman Clarke first learned to play drums at a children's-home in Pittsburgh. He then started to play professionally in St Louis and Cincinnati as a teenager and moved to New York in 1935. By 1938 he was in a band led by saxophonist Teddy Hill with Dizzy Gillespie on trumpet. Hill gave Clarke the nickname 'Klook-a-mop' in mimicry of his assymetrical drum patterns. In 1941, with Hill now manager at Minton's Playhouse, Clarke led the house band that included pianist Thelonious Monk. He juggled the job with work for Louis Armstrong's big band and with Ella Fitzgerald, being widely popular for his listening skills and lightness of touch.

Kenny Clarke was crucial to the liberation of the snare and bass drums from simply time-keeping roles – he let the ride-cymbal beat and hi-hat accents take care of those – allowing drummers to play more polyrhythmically and comment more freely on the unfolding events around them. Bebop bands thus became more agile, flexible and responsive.

Clarke worked with almost all the leading figures of bebop in the 1940s and '50s before relocating to France in 1956 to play, teach and co-lead the multi-national Kenny Clarke-Francy Boland Big Band.

MILES DAVIS *(1926–1991)*

Miles Dewey Davis III was one of the bebop pioneers in the 1940s but, like a jazz-playing Picasso, he subsequently moved through several creative periods, from bop to orchestral jazz, and from modal jazz and the borders of free form to jazz-rock fusion in his later years. The son of a St Louis dentist, Davis moved to New York in 1944 to study trumpet at the Juilliard School, rooming and playing with Charlie Parker. He then reacted against bebop's intensity to work on a more spacious and delicately nuanced jazz in the 'Birth of the Cool' nine-piece in 1949–50. Narcotics stalled his career but he made an acclaimed comeback at the 1955 Newport Jazz Festival. He formed a superb hard bop quintet that included saxophonist John Coltrane in 1955, recorded 'Kind of Blue' – one of the all-time great jazz albums – with Coltrane and others in 1959, and subsequently went on to work on large-scale jazz concertos with composer and arranger Gil Evans, and led a series of influential small groups from the 1960s to the '80s.

DIZZY GILLESPIE *(1917–1993)*

John Birks 'Dizzy' Gillespie taught himself trombone and trumpet from the age of 12 after the early death of his father. He acquired theory as well as technique, and his trumpet idol was the swing virtuoso Roy Eldridge – an influence that won him a job as Eldridge's replacement in saxophonist Teddy

Hill's big-band in 1937. Gillespie then worked in Cabell 'Cab' Calloway's expert but highly showbiz-oriented band, and when Hill became manager at Minton's Playhouse, the young trumpeter regularly attended the late-night jam sessions from which bebop emerged. Gillespie's trumpet skills and original insights into harmony made him a significant figure in bebop's evolution, and in 1945 a quintet he co-led with Charlie Parker produced the first of the method's enduring themes, including 'Salt Peanuts' and 'Hot House'. From 1946 to 1950, Gillespie led a big-band merging swing, bebop and Afro-Cuban music and his effervescence, musicality and humour brought him constant work in various line-ups from the 1950s until his final active months at the end of 1992.

THELONIOUS MONK *(1917–1982)*

Born at Rocky Mount, North Carolina, in 1917, Thelonious Sphere Monk moved with his family to New York in early childhood, and studied piano from the age of ten. Rooted at first in the stride style, he played New York rent parties, organ and piano in Baptist churches, and spent two years on the road accompanying a faith-healing evangelist. Back in New York

Thelonious Monk played like a drummer as much as a pianist, but his dissonantly crushed harmonies were starkly eloquent. His compositions 'Epistrophy', 'Crepuscule with Nellie' and 'Round Midnight' became standard jazz themes.

in 1937, Monk was eventually hired by Kenny Clarke for the house band at Minton's. Monk worked closely with regular Minton's sitters-in Dizzy Gillespie and Charlie Christian, and he encouraged an emerging young pianist, Bud Powell. Monk worked with Miles Davis, Sonny Rollins and John Coltrane in the 1950s, and left a unique legacy as one of the most important American composers of the 20th century, regardless of genre.

CHARLIE PARKER *(1920–1955)*

Charles 'Charlie' Parker, Jr was born in Kansas City, his vaudeville-performer father left home when his son was 11 and his mother Addie worked nights as a cleaner, which allowed Parker to work nights of his own – hanging out in the Kansas nightclubs from his mid-teens, listening to the great jazz saxophonists, most particularly Kansas City hero Lester Young. His improvisations were shaped like Young's, but were played much faster and with more passing and incidental notes. Swing bandleader Jay McShann hired Parker in 1938 (he then acquired the nickname 'Yardbird' or just 'Bird'), and his exceptional melodic memory gelled with Dizzy Gillespie's understanding of chords in the Harlem late-night jam sessions.

After sometimes painful onstage experimentation, Charlie Parker became so much at ease in all keys that he could stray from one to another and return to the tune without getting lost.

From 1945, Parker and Gillespie began producing new jazz of an audacity and excitement to rival that of Louis Armstrong's Hot Fives and Sevens. For producer Ross Russell's Dial label between February 1946 and December 1947 Parker produced variations on stunning originals, including 'Yardbird Suite', 'Ornithology' and 'Moose The Mooche', and even shambolic performances of haunting expressiveness, such as his disorientated performance of 'Lover Man'. Despite a six-month hospitalisation for a mental breakdown in 1946–7 and continuing problems with drugs, he recorded magnificent music, including work with a classical string quartet and with Afro-Cuban line-ups. He died suddenly at 34, in the apartment of his patron and friend, Rothschild family-member Nica de Koenigswarter, on 12 March 1955. When the news broke in New York, graffiti artists scrawled 'Bird Lives!' on the city's walls.

MAX ROACH *(1924–2007)*

Apart from Kenny Clarke, the other significant drummer of the first wave of the bebop movement was Maxwell Lemuel 'Max' Roach. His mother was a gospel singer, and the young Max played both piano and drums for church functions. Roach became resident drummer at Clark Monroe's Uptown House in Harlem in 1942, and played in the bebop-nurturing jam sessions both there and at Minton's. Roach made his first recordings with Coleman Hawkins, and subsequently played with Parker's quintet in its most creative period from 1947–9. In the 1950s, Roach co-founded a definitive quintet of the pungent new hard bop style with trumpeter Clifford Brown, Bud Powell's pianist brother Richie, saxophonist Harold Land and subsequently Sonny Rollins. Its immensely creative two-year life ended when a car accident killed Brown and Powell. Roach became active in the Civil Rights movement and he played and composed into his seventies, exploring forms from Chinese traditional music to hip-hop in later years.

Max Roach advanced the lighter, cymbal-oriented groove and a looser, off-beat creativity with accents, and he was also an unusually tuneful percussionist who paid close attention to the tonal potential of different parts of the kit.

THE BIGGER PICTURE
OTHER KEY CONTRIBUTORS TO BEBOP

Bebop was predominantly a small-ensemble music, but Dizzy Gillespie's 1947 orchestra and the 1949 Birth of the Cool band revealed its larger-scale potential. Some swing stars were also open to it, including pianist Earl Hines and vocalist Billy Eckstine, and bandleaders Woody Herman and Stan Kenton. Woodrow Charles 'Woody' Herman (1913–1987) had emerged in 1923 as the 'Boy Wonder of the Clarinet' in his parents' vaudeville act, worked with and then inherited songwriter Isham Jones' popular orchestra and had a million-selling success with 'Woodchoppers' Ball' in 1939. After World War II, Herman ran a succession of orchestras he called The Herds –with contributions from leading composers and arrangers and strong soloists, including the gifted and melodic teenage saxophonist Stan Getz. Stanley Newcomb 'Stan' Kenton (1911–1979), who had formed his first orchestra in 1940, was also open-minded and alert to new music. Kenton's work often reflected both classical music and what he liked to call 'progressive' jazz. His huge bands became very popular, and gifted bop-oriented musicians such as saxophonists Lee Konitz and Art Pepper were among his soloists.

Thelonious Monk protegé Earl Randolph 'Bud' Powell (1924–1966) was one of the most creative of the first generation bebop pianists – a young master of the demanding swing styles of Art

Tatum and Teddy Wilson whose mature style emulated the headlong momentum of bebop's leading sax and trumpet stars, and who regularly played with Parker, Gillespie and others. Powell was dogged by mental health problems, but he worked productively through the 1950s (such themes as 'Tempus Fugue-It' and 'Glass Enclosure' also testified to his gifts as a composer). Mary Lou Williams (1910–1981) was also a prodigious pianistic and composing talent, who helped bring Andy Kirk's Clouds of Joy band to national fame in the 1930s, composed for Duke Ellington and Benny Goodman, and arranged for Dizzy Gillespie. Her 'Zodiac Suite' was performed by the New York Philharmonic Orchestra in 1945. Williams' piano style bridged swing and bebop, and she was also a significant role model for women instrumentalists in jazz.

Other notable figures of the early years of bebop included three formidable saxophonists in Dexter Gordon, Wardell Gray and Sonny Stitt. Tenor saxophonist Gordon was a disciple of Coleman Hawkins and Lester Young who added Charlie Parker's innovations to the mix; Gray was an Earl Hines and Benny Goodman sideman with an advanced bebop sensibility; Edward 'Sonny' Stitt was a prodigiously skilful alto saxophonist devoted to Charlie Parker and taught by Gray. The short-lived Theodore 'Fats' Navarro was one of the best of all Gillespie-inspired bebop trumpeters, whose career was cut short by his early death from tuberculosis in 1950. Navarro was a major influence on the phrasing of trombonist James Louis

'JJ' Johnson, a remarkable technician who showed how bebop's speed could be accommodated on his most stately instrument. Johnson played in the Birth of the Cool band, Gillespie's orchestra and with many leading beboppers.

Bob Brookmeyer also developed an agile method using a trumpet-like valve trombone rather than the traditionally slide-equipped instrument.

Inspired by Charlie Christian, a number of virtuosic guitarists evolved styles compatible with the new music – most notably the elegantly swinging Wes Montgomery (whose soft sound derived from plucking notes with his thumb rather than a pick), the lyrical Jim Hall, and the bluesy Kenny Burrell. Singers who could handle bebop's hairpin-turns and zigzags included the Lionel Hampton band's Betty Carter (Hampton called her 'Betty Bebop'), Sheila Jordan and former drummer Dave Lambert, who recorded on vocals with Charlie Parker and went on to co-found the famous Lambert, Hendricks and Ross vocal trio. Bebop-oriented double-bassists included Ray Brown, Percy Heath and Charles Mingus, and a dynamic group of drummers emerged, including Art Blakey, Philly Joe Jones, Shelly Manne and Roy Haynes.

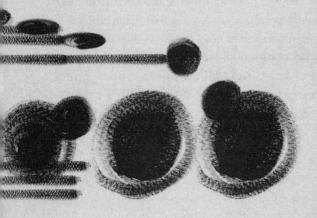

6

VISIONARIES –
THE COOL SCHOOL,
HARD BOP AND
FREE JAZZ

Jazz methods changed fast in the 1940s and '50s – from the quietly bebop-like, classically influenced sound of The Cool School to the sermonising energy of hard bop, and on to the uncompromising, uninhibited and sometimes unstructured music of free jazz. Rock and roll took over jazz's formerly big audiences in this period, but each of these styles had loyal fans and extensively advanced the music as an art.

FROM '50s COOL TO COLTRANE'S FIRE

MODERN JAZZ QUARTET (MJQ)

The Modern Jazz Quartet (MJQ) began life as the rhythm section in Dizzy Gillespie's late 1940s' bands, but became one of the best-loved and longest running of all small jazz groups, active for over 30 years. The first 1952 line-up featured vibraphonist Milt Jackson, pianist John Lewis (who also wrote music for the 'Birth of the Cool' sessions), bassist Percy Heath and pioneering bebop drummer Kenny Clarke – delicate percussionist Connie Kay replaced Clarke three years later. A defining band of the post-bebop Cool School, the MJQ played with the refinement of a chamber ensemble, and used such classical forms as fugues and rondos while retaining an unmistakable jazz feeling, particularly in Jackson's crisp swing and blues phrasing. The group flourished until Jackson quit in 1974, but reconvened for reunion tours until the late 1980s.

LENNIE TRISTANO *(1919–1978)*

Leonard Joseph 'Lennie' Tristano first studied piano with his opera singer mother, then learned piano, wind instruments and theory at a school for the blind in the 1930s. He developed his own advanced bebop theories after graduating from Chicago's American Conservatory of Music in 1943. Tristano played with Charlie Parker and Dizzy Gillespie, but his perception of bebop was more laid-back and avoided emotional extremes. Tristano's knowledge, curiosity and rigour made him a hard taskmaster but an illuminating teacher. Saxophonists Lee Konitz and Warne Marsh were among his star pupils, as was pianist Bill Evans – who brought Tristano's purity and precision to his own work and particularly to Miles Davis's landmark jazz session 'Kind of Blue'.

DAVE BRUBECK *(1920–2012)*

Pianist David Warren 'Dave' Brubeck's hugely popular music caused controversy in the 1950s between jazz purists who disliked his use of European classical forms and admirers entranced by it. Brubeck studied with classical composer Darius Milhaud, and formed his first quartet in 1951 with a soft-toned Cool School alto saxophonist, Paul Desmond. The quartet's self-made 'Jazz at Oberlin' was

Rancher's son Dave Brubeck majored as a vet, before switching to music in 1939.

widely admired, and with the dazzlingly inventive drummer Joe Morello and African American bassist Eugene Wright (Brubeck always resisted segregationist pressures on his choice of sidemen) he formed his most famous quartet. Creative use of unusual time signatures coupled with infectious swing and arresting solos made them a global success. Brubeck confounded his early critics by becoming greatly respected as a composer and an inspirational innovator in rhythm; in his later years he wrote ballet and symphonic music, various cantatas and a mass, and continued to perform into his eighties.

BILL EVANS *(1929–1980)*

He was one of the most light-stepping and unassuming of jazz maestros, but the pianist William John Evans, known as Bill Evans, left a very big footprint on the work of the jazz pianists that came after him – notably Herbie Hancock, McCoy Tyner, Chick Corea and Keith Jarrett. He learned piano, violin and flute as a child, absorbed the jazz piano ideas of both Bud Powell and Lennie Tristano, and significantly influenced Miles Davis's 'Kind of Blue'. Evans' 1960s' group, with the ingeniously counter-melodic double-bassist Scott LaFaro and the drummer Paul Motian, established a model for innumerable jazz piano trios to come. His compositions 'Blue In Green' and 'Waltz For Debby' continue to be reinterpreted all over the world.

GIL EVANS *(1912–1988)*

The collaboration between Miles Davis and Canadian composer and arranger Ian Ernest Gilmore 'Gil' Evans from the 1940s to the '60s was a relationship comparable in intimacy and outcomes to that of Duke Ellington and his soloists. Evans had educated himself musically by listening to jazz records and poring over classical scores in libraries. Once in New York in the 1940s, he worked as a staff arranger for Claude Thornhill's sophisticated dance band, adding French horns, tuba and woodwinds to produce ethereal effects that were memorably dubbed 'clouds of sound'. These were the raw materials of the 'Birth of the Cool' band when Evans, Miles Davis and Thornhill saxists Gerry Mulligan and Lee Konitz met to discuss ways out of the bebop labyrinth in Evans' apartment in 1948. Avoiding jazz clichés, substituting tone-colour for riffs, Evans developed the unique orchestral sound that he deployed in various ways throughout a long working life.

THEODORE WALTER 'SONNY' ROLLINS *(1930–)*

Saxophonist Theodore Walter 'Sonny' Rollins shared a Harlem childhood with Duke Ellington, Coleman Hawkins and Thelonious Monk as neighbours and kindred spirits. He worked with Miles Davis in the early 1950s, enjoyed practice sessions with Ornette Coleman – and long sabbaticals in which he would withdraw to study and practise. Rollins merged the speed of Charlie Parker, the gravitas of Coleman Hawkins and the lyricism of Lester Young. The terse conviction with which he fused those influences made him an early hero of the hard bop style in a powerful mid-1950s' band featuring drummer Max Roach and trumpeter Clifford Brown (ended by a car accident that killed Brown and pianist Richie Powell). He then steered close to free jazz in the early '60s with Ornette Coleman associates Don Cherry (pocket trumpet) and Billy Higgins (drums) plus Jim Hall (guitar). He took a three-year lay-off at the end of the decade, and then came back with the more accessible repertoire of standard songs, funk and calypsos that entertained big audiences worldwide for the rest of his working life – often in the unbroken two-hour shows he continued to play into his eighties.

ORNETTE COLEMAN *(1930–)*

Saxophonist (and occasional trumpeter and violinist) Ornette Coleman was often treated as a charlatan or an incompetent innocent when he began playing professionally in the 1950s, because he idiosyncratically strayed across keys, and didn't feel bound by the chord sequences of songs. But the self-taught saxophonist was developing a freer way of improvising, deploying looser guidelines than had been used in jazz before. When he formed a West Coast band including bassist Charlie Haden and trumpeter Don Cherry (later father to contemporary singers Neneh and Eagle-Eye Cherry), he found his ideal partners. Coleman's 1950s' and '60s' music was sometimes loosely bebop-like, very blues-influenced, and allowed harmonies, melodies and rhythms to unpredictably develop and change during performance – a reflexive kind of jazz-making that would alter the course of the music. A unique improviser, with a voice-like sound and a torrent of spontaneous ideas, he was also an exceptional composer. In later years, Coleman wrote symphonies, worked with dancers and opera singers, and contributed to the jazz-fusion electric approach in the 1970s with another highly influential band, Prime Time.

JOHN COLTRANE *(1926–1967)*

John William Coltrane died in 1967 at only 40, but his achievements had already set him on the way to becoming one of the most influential musicians in jazz. Coltrane was born in North Carolina in 1926, played R&B in the 1950s and worked with Dizzy Gillespie, Hammond organist Jimmy Smith, Thelonious Monk and Miles Davis (the latter relationship culminating in the great 'Kind of Blue' sessions). Coltrane pushed bebop to the outer limits

Coltrane broke new ground for the saxophone, was a gifted composer and an indefatigably driven expressive artist whose work reached beyond the jazz audience to every kind of open-minded listener.

of speed and harmonic complexity. His contemplative, mantra-like 'A Love Supreme' became a hit with both jazz and progressive rock listeners in 1964. He rescued the lighter soprano saxophone and gave it a creative identity only previously achieved by Sidney Bechet. His later groups turned jazz performances into intensely emotional trance-like states, echoing the African religious rituals at the roots of the music's origins.

John Coltrane investigated the saxophone's

overtones

to play beyond its designed range and with several notes at once commonly termed

'multiphonics'.

He used a scale-based modal approach and set a new standard for small-band improvising with the revolutionary quartet featuring pianist McCoy Tyner, bassist Jimmy Garrison and drummer Elvin Jones.

THE BIGGER PICTURE
OTHER KEY CONTRIBUTORS TO THE COOL SCHOOL, HARD BOP AND FREE

When the Cool School was popular and influential in the 1950s, one of its most charismatic figures was the trumpeter Chesney Henry 'Chet' Baker (1929–1998), whose playing could be as soft as a sigh, or swing with an unhurried ease, and who sang in a seductively vulnerable crooner's tones. With former 'Birth of the Cool' baritone saxophonist and composer Gerry Mulligan, Baker founded an unusual piano-less quartet whose dreamily winding, harmonically porous lyricism made it a favourite in the 1950s' jazz polls. Other influential creators of the cool West Coast jazz sound included the advanced trumpeter 'Shorty' Rogers (Milton Michael Rajonsky), who adapted 20th-century classical techniques to jazz, and also saxophonists Jimmy Giuffre and Bud Shank, bassist and bandleader Curtis Counce, and drummers Shelly Manne and Frank Butler.

The dominance of the Cool School was challenged by the muscle and intensity of the hard boppers, and the uncompromising fearlessness of the free players, who sought to jettison chord structures and song forms. In 1953, fiery drummer Art Blakey and subtly funky Cape Verdean pianist Horace Silver were the original founders of the Jazz Messengers, which became the most famous of all hard bop groups. Under Blakey's later leadership, the band introduced rising stars of the hard bop movement such as saxophonists Jackie McLean, Johnny Griffin, Benny Golson and Wayne Shorter, trumpeters Lee Morgan, Freddie Hubbard, Woody Shaw and Wynton Marsalis, and pianists Bobby Timmons and Cedar Walton.

Hard bop lengthened solos whilst making compositions more cryptic, and rekindled popular jazz links with African American church music and the blues. Free jazz could also be rootsy, but its popular appeal was more limited, and its structures and materials often very different. An innovator as radical as Ornette Coleman or John Coltrane was the pianist Cecil Taylor, whose music seethed with fast-moving references from 20th-century classical composers like Stravinsky, Bartók and Elliott Carter as well as the ideas of Thelonious Monk, Bud Powell and Dave Brubeck. Taylor's musical dialogues with the ballet star Mikhail Baryshnikov are among his most remarkable achievements. Other powerful originals of the first free jazz generation were the American saxophonists Albert Ayler, Archie Shepp, Steve Lacy, Jimmy Lyons and Pharoah Sanders, and the Dane John Tchicai, trombonist Roswell Rudd, and drummers Milford Graves and Sunny Murray. Later in the 1960s, other schools of free playing coalesced around the Association for the Advancement of Creative Musicians (AACM) in Chicago, the Jazz Composers' Orchestra Association (JCOA) and the collective associated

Cecil Taylor once said his aim was to make piano music that imitates 'the leaps in space a dancer makes'.

with the keyboardist and composer Sonny Blount, better known as Sun Ra. Sun Ra built the long-running band he called the Arkestra from a loyal group of creative soloists, much as Duke Ellington did. He released many albums on his own Saturn label, that combined early electronic technology (he was one of the first successful improvising soloists on the Moog synthesiser) with swing band arrangements, rough-edged and collective free-jazz soloing and very powerful percussion.

The 1950s and '60s saw new styles of jazz emerge, and eventually find their own devoted audiences. Some of the most inventive composers found ways to bring all this new diversity together. George Russell was a revolutionary musical theoretician who provided the analytical basis for much of the cyclical, scale-based modal jazz that superseded bebop, through the exhaustively detailed study he named *The Lydian Chromatic Concept of Tonal Organisation*. Russell was the son of a music professor, and had been a bebop drummer in the 1940s, but he began his investigations into alternative jazz methods whilst hospitalised for tuberculosis in that decade. He wrote audacious style-crossing themes including 'Cubano Be, Cubano Bop' (for Dizzy Gillespie) and 'A Bird In Igor's Yard' (as a bow to both Charlie Parker and Igor Stravinsky), and drew a superb Bill Evans piano performance on 'Concerto for Billy The

Kid' for the brilliant album 'Jazz Workshop' in 1956. Russell hired many fine soloists including saxophonist Eric Dolphy and vocalist Sheila Jordan in the 1960s, then worked in Scandinavia with an emerging young European jazz star, saxophonist Jan Garbarek. An even bigger presence as a composer was Charles Mingus, who was a virtuoso double-bassist too. Inspired by Duke Ellington (and considered by many to be his true heir), Mingus developed an Ellington-like approach to composing in real time with his soloists, he had hard bop affiliations in foregrounding blues and gospel music, but juggled uninhibitedly with abrupt tempo changes and free-collective improvisations.

Mingus could make his orchestras shout and swing like Count Basie, but he also gave them Duke Ellington's sumptuous tone colours and layered textures. He saw the jazz ensemble as a vehicle for both collective and individual expressiveness, and he fearlessly allowed his players to float freely in and out of the written parts. The raucously spontaneous feel of a Mingus orchestra was quite different to the machine-like orderliness of much big-band jazz. His loose approach was to have a huge influence on subsequent jazz composition; notably in the work of Carla Bley and in new jazz orchestras emerging in the present era.

7 VISIONARIES –
FUSION AND
CONTEMPORARY

Synthesisers, bass guitars and funk rhythms brought changes to jazz after the 1960s. But, from then to now, so have the folk songs of old Europe, the dance grooves of Afrobeat, or the intricacies of Asian and Latin American rhythms. Jazz, the hungry transformer of any and every musical sound, continues to change and grow.

SOME PROPHETS OF JAZZ TODAY

HERBIE HANCOCK *(1940–)*

Herbert Jeffrey 'Herbie' Hancock began piano lessons at the age of seven and was playing Mozart in public with the Chicago Symphony Orchestra four years later. He joined the Blue Note record label in his early twenties, and his 1962 debut album 'Takin' Off' included the catchy original 'Watermelon Man', which became a pop hit for Cuban percussionist Mongo Santamaria. Hancock's inclusiveness – he drew creatively and equally on jazz, classical music, pop and later electronics – made him a cornerstone of Miles Davis's great mid-1960s quintet. Alongside his jazz stardom he became a successful soul and pop artist with his funk band Headhunters in the 1970s and the electro-disco chart hit 'Rockit' in 1983. A brilliant improviser and a natural collaborator, Hancock has treated any idiomatic challenge as an invitation to create something special. He has worked with singers from Christina Aguilera to Paul Simon and Annie Lennox, won a Grammy for his Joni Mitchell album 'Rivers' and is one of the most widely sampled of all jazz composers by DJs, hip-hop artists and producers.

JOE ZAWINUL *(1932–2007)*

Vienna-born Josef Erich 'Joe' Zawinul was a lynchpin of Weather Report, one of the most creative bands in 1970s and '80s jazz-rock fusion. He studied classical music at Vienna's conservatoire and jazz at Boston's Berklee Music School in the United States from 1959. He wrote the jazz and soul hit 'Mercy, Mercy, Mercy' for an early employer, gospel-influenced hard bop saxophonist Julian 'Cannonball' Adderley, and then the brooding tapestry 'In a Silent Way' in 1969, for Miles Davis's pioneering electric jazz album of the same name. In 1970, Zawinul launched Weather Report with Davis's saxophonist Wayne Shorter and the group made 17 albums, ran for 15 years and created several enduring themes – most notably the jubilant, rhythmically capricious 'Birdland'. In his later years, Zawinul developed Weather Report's methods further in the stylistically eclectic Zawinul Syndicate.

PAT METHENY *(1954–)*

Jazz musicians are sometimes criticised for writing tunes that can't be sung, but the Missouri guitarist Patrick Bruce

'Pat' Metheny has consistently achieved the opposite, whilst remaining a consummate musician who has never dumbed jazz down. A teenage prodigy, Metheny had influential early experiences alongside the great vibraphonist Gary Burton and bass guitar maestro Jaco Pastorius, before his growing popularity led him to form his longest-running and best-loved ensemble – the Pat Metheny Group (or PMG) – in 1977. But he continued to resist comfort zones, working with free jazz pioneer Ornette Coleman (notably on 'Song X' in 1985), the minimalist composer Steve Reich ('Different Trains' in 1987), and with artists as different as the flintily abstract British guitarist Derek Bailey as well as Herbie Hancock and the late Michael Brecker. He also invented a huge multi-instrumental one-man band 'Orchestrion' and creatively developed the voice-like sound of the electronic Synclavier, and the acoustic guitar palette with the multi-stringed Pikasso harp-guitar.

JAN GARBAREK *(1947–)*

Norwegian saxophonist Jan Garbarek was inspired to play by hearing John Coltrane on the radio as a teenager, and then passed through the fire of a raw, Albert Ayler-inspired free jazz sound and on to his own delicately nuanced approach, influenced by his homeland's folk themes, the *joik* vocal styles (traditional singing of the Sami people) of the Arctic Circle and music from Asia. Garbarek became one of the first recruits to German producer Manfred Eicher's new ECM record label, founded to document independent new European development. Through a series of diversely cross-cultural ventures in the 1970s, Garbarek moved between spaciously atmospheric, explicitly jazzy and sparingly funky music. But it was with the 'Officium' session of 1993, when he improvised around hymns, Gregorian chants and mediaeval polyphonies sung by the classical Hilliard Ensemble, that Garbarek found himself part of a million-selling success story. He continued to work with the Hilliards until 2014.

WAYNE SHORTER *(1933–)*

Like his former boss, Miles Davis, saxophonist Wayne Shorter's charisma embraced a sparingly eloquent instrumental sound that many struggled to copy, a one-touch group empathy that countless bandleaders strove to unpick, and an enigmatic personal style (he was 'Mr Weird' in high school) that seemed to mirror the blend of mystery and muscle in his music. Shorter's composing skills, and his terse and pungent saxophone variations made him a key figure in Art Blakey's Jazz Messengers from 1959 to 1963. He was also pivotal to the Miles Davis quintet of the mid-1960s, and then the co-founder of the groundbreaking fusion band Weather Report. Shorter's themes added fresh inflections to the blues and new metrical twists to the familiar paths of hard bop, and he became one of the outstanding jazz composers of the late 20th century. The quartet he began leading as he approached his seventies has gained wide acclaim, both for Shorter's continuing inventiveness as a composer and the conversational vitality of its collective playing.

KEITH JARRETT *(1945–)*

A single performance lasting little more than an hour, on a faulty piano at a midnight show whilst wearing a back brace and suffering from travel fatigue and exasperation turned the then 29-year-old American pianist Keith Jarrett into that rare jazz phenomenon – a household name. 'The Köln Concert' – the recording of Jarrett's hypnotic and lyrical all-improvised set in the Köln Opera House in January 1975 – has sold over three million copies, but the former classical child prodigy from Pennsylvania had already made a distinctive impact in jazz circles, as a sideman for Art Blakey, Miles Davis and saxophonist Charles Lloyd in the 1960s, and with his own compositionally vigorous quartets early in the next decade. Jarrett's technique, improviser's instincts and love of song-like melody have made his work widely accessible yet full of surprises. His 1970s' small-band work with Ornette Coleman associates Dewey Redman (saxophones) and Charlie Haden (bass), and subsequently the European Quartet including Jan Garbarek, has been almost as influential on contemporary bandleaders as his playing has been on pianists. Moreover, his Standards Trio (formed in

1983) rekindled interest in American standard songs and Bill Evans-inspired piano-trio jazz. The prolific Jarrett has also performed organ recitals and classical concertos, and has only ever been slowed down by the two-year withdrawal forced on him by chronic fatigue syndrome in the late 1990s.

ABDULLAH IBRAHIM [DOLLAR BRAND] *(1934–)*

Under his adopted Muslim name of Abdullah Ibrahim, Adolph Johannes Brand has gracefully moved into his eighties as one of the most respected figures of South African music. Ibrahim worked with trumpeter Hugh Masekela, saxophonist Kippie Moeketsi and others in the hard boppish Jazz Epistles group during South Africa's oppressive apartheid era, but as the regime's brutality increased, he left for Switzerland and then, with Duke Ellington's help, the United States. A fascinating alchemist of township dances, African Methodist hymns and the jazz of Ellington and Thelonious Monk, Ibrahim went on to compose some of the most memorable of recent jazz themes. He has continued to write new musical impressions of his homeland and his travels, and revisit his much-loved themes – sometimes solo, in reverentially meditative recitals, sometimes in delicate group performances uncannily echoing Duke Ellington's.

Adolph Johannes Brand was nicknamed 'Dollar' in his teens, for the deals he struck with American sailors to buy jazz records in the Cape Town docks.

CARLA BLEY *(1936–)*

Born Lovella May Borg, in California, Carla Bley was encouraged to learn the piano by her choirmaster father and began playing in Bay Area clubs. On moving to New York at 17 in 1953, she worked as a cigarette salesgirl at the Birdland jazz club. She met and married the Canadian pianist Paul Bley, studied briefly with George Russell, wrote quirky pieces that were recorded by Russell, Paul Bley and trumpeter Art Farmer, and became involved in the 1960s' experiments in cooperative promotion that led to the formation of the New York Jazz Composer's Orchestra. She wrote the suite 'A Genuine Tong Funeral' for vibraphonist Gary Burton and arranged Spanish Civil War songs for Ornette Coleman bassist Charlie Haden's Liberation Music Orchestra. She wrote music for Keith Jarrett, toured with Cream bassist Jack Bruce's rock group, composed tributes to Nino Rota, Kurt Weill and Thelonious Monk, and became increasingly in demand as a writer of both jazz and contemporary-classical music from her mid-life onward.

HANDFULS OF KEYS

Despite advanced keyboard technology, the conventional piano has maintained its central role in jazz. Great American pianists including Herbie Hancock, Keith Jarrett, Chick Corea, McCoy Tyner and the octogenarian Ahmad Jamal (a Miles Davis favourite in the 1950s) have continued to shine into the 21st century. Newer originals have included the melodically ingenious Brad Mehldau, the culture-crossing and rhythmically advanced Asian-American Vijay Iyer and the Cecil Taylor-inspired avantists Myra Melford and Marilyn Crispell. Gifted younger Europeans include the German Michael Wollny, the Pole Leszek Możdżer, the Finn Iiro Rantala, the German Julia Hülsmann and the Briton Gwilym Simcock.

THE BIGGER PICTURE
OTHER KEY FIGURES OF CONTEMPORARY JAZZ

THE CLASSIC TRADITION AND WYNTON MARSALIS
The most famous advocate of jazz displaying explicit American roots, Wynton Marsalis is a multi-stylistic trumpeter of flawless technique, who became the charismatic jazz boss at New York's Lincoln Center for the Performing Arts in 1987 and globe-trotting leader of its orchestra. As willing to demonstrate jazz values in a struggling inner-city school as he is in Carnegie Hall, Marsalis is also a prolific composer for ensembles from jazz bands and choirs to symphony orchestras. Many other classy artists also cherish American jazz traditions in their own ways, like the swing devoted saxophonists Scott Hamilton (a former Benny Goodman sideman) and the elegant Harry Allen.

HORN FANFARE – SOME CELEBRITIES OF POST-BOP
The catch-all term post-bop can embrace a swathe of styles from classic bebop to free jazz. Saxophones are often dominant in it, and key figures have included the powerful Coltrane-ist David Murray, the short-lived virtuoso Michael Brecker, the formidable Joe Lovano and Dave Liebman, and Wynton Marsalis's brother Branford. The 'Saxophone Colossus', Sonny Rollins, continued his tempestuous saxophone marathons into his eighties and the versatile Charles Lloyd came out of a mid-

life retirement in the 1990s to re-establish himself as a soulful developer of the methods of John Coltrane.

THE SINGERS, NOT THE SONGS

Classic Broadway songs, blues, folk songs and pop-inflected music are all being reworked by innovative singers today, including Dianne Reeves, Bobby McFerrin, Kurt Elling, Cassandra Wilson, Diana Krall, and latterly the young New Yorker Gretchen Parlato and the popular Esperanza Spalding (also a fine double-bassist). The English singer Norma Winstone and the Italian Diana Torto are among leading European explorers of more experimental approaches.

THINKING BIG – AMERICAN ORCHESTRAL JAZZ

Among contemporary jazz composers, Carla Bley continued her imperturbably idiosyncratic way, and Minnesota-born Maria Schneider led large ensembles with spacious, painterly music that developed the legacy of her mentor Gil Evans. The exciting Mingus Big Band continued to tour the great music of its namesake, who died in 1979. At the other end of the timeline, New York-based Canadian Darcy James Argue has used unusual instruments and culture-crossing composing techniques in his radical 'steampunk' big band, the Secret Society.

GUITAR HEROES

Swing and bebop guitar star Charlie Christian inspired a generation of disciples in the 1950s, including Wes Montgomery and Jim Hall – and they spawned their own successors, such as John McLaughlin, Bill Frisell, John Scofield, Emily Remler and Wolfgang Muthspiel. Briton McLaughlin, originally a flamenco and blues enthusiast and Django Reinhardt fan, stunned listeners with his pithy phrasing in Miles Davis's late-1960s' bands, and subsequently his Indian-influenced Mahavishnu Orchestra and Shakti groups, and is still in torrential flow today. More of a sound collagist than McLaughlin is the equally influential Bill Frisell – a former Jim Hall student who has used advanced electronics to glue country music, jazz and rock seamlessly together, and interpret the work of American composers from Aaron Copland, Charles Ives and Muddy Waters to Bob Dylan and even Madonna.

EUROPEAN STORIES

Norway's Jan Garbarek remained Europe's best-known jazz-inspired artist, but Polish trumpeter Tomasz Stańko, French multi-instrumentalist Louis Sclavis, double-bassist Henri Texier, and the British reeds player John Surman have all revealed fascinating inspirations – from France and north Africa in the work of Sclavis and Texier, from Polish folk-songs and classical music in Stańko's, from English folk and choral traditions in Surman's. The late Swedish pianist and composer Esbjörn Svensson's work also reached a worldwide audience through a chemistry of invitingly song-like themes, jazz spontaneity and rock theatricality. British keyboardist Django Bates and his spirited circle collectively ran a unique 21-piece orchestra in Loose Tubes – vivaciously active from 1984–1990, and reunited in 2014. The Canadian expatriate trumpeter and composer Kenny Wheeler (prolifically active until his death in 2014) entranced audiences with a mix of wistful melodies and robust orchestral-jazz and improv treatments. His UK contemporary, Stan Tracey, gave Thelonious Monk's and Duke Ellington's ideas his own truculently witty spin. British composers Colin Towns and Michael Gibbs have also absorbingly explored fusions of the Duke Ellington and Gil Evans tradition, post-bop and rock. Caribbean rhythms, and tunes drawn from reggae and ska, have been brought into British jazz by a number of artists with West Indian roots, most notably the saxophonist and bandleader Courtney Pine, a virtuoso performer with a personal mission to bring the jazz tradition to the widest possible audience. Dance rhythms and electronics also broadened the jazz palette in the hands of such explorers as the Norwegians Arve Henriksen and Nils Petter Molvaer (trumpeters with strong identities as composers) and the resourceful collective Jaga Jazzist.

ON THE MARGINS
GENRE-BENDING AND THE AVANT GARDE

After the rise of free jazz in the 1960s, it was not uncommon to find some listeners walking out of experimental gigs in protest when the going got too tough. But by the 1990s, even the most extreme experiments were coming to be more widely accepted. In an instantly interconnected world, a raft of 20th-century innovation including contemporary-classical and serial music, folk traditions from many cultures, electronics, homemade instruments, *musique concrete*, sound-collagism, ambience, post-punk and computer music was becoming readily available to musicians and listeners alike. Jazz players, always instinctive appropriators of interesting ideas, have enthusiastically helped themselves.

And with them, in recent times, niche audiences have blossomed and found each other. They have discovered such unclassifiable performers as New Yorker John Zorn, originally a blistering free jazz saxophonist who developed as a unique composer, fascinated by devising liberating game-like structures for improvisers, and also by radical reappraisal of traditional

Jewish music. Or Dave Douglas, a gifted trumpeter close to Zorn's circle, who applied his jazz fluency to contemporary-classical music, free improv and folk forms. Older progressives drawing on the African American influence on the free jazz of the 1960s have also continued to develop into their senior years – like player/composers Henry Threadgill, Anthony Braxton and Roscoe Mitchell, or the Miles Davis-influenced trumpeter Wadada Leo Smith.

Free-thinking younger artists now include American saxophonists and composers Steve Coleman (a mystic guided by the symbolism associated with some world-music rhythms), Steve Lehman (who uses computer sound-analysis in his pieces) and John O'Gallagher (a former classical saxophonist absorbed in George Russell's modal theories). European improv saxophonists Peter Brötzmann and Evan Parker, percussionist Han Bennink and pianist Alex von Schlippenbach have steadily swapped their *enfant terrible* reputations for widespread respect, and in Australia, improvising trio The Necks play a popular all-improvised blend of hypnotically looping ambient music and jazz. Energetic New York trio The Bad Plus create rampant jazz makeovers of pop hits and classical themes, and Britain's Polar Bear rhythmically fascinating conjunctions of free jazz, electronics and world-music. The contemporaneity, compelling rhythms and jump-cut energy of hip-hop creatively affected new jazz, notably through the popular work of the Herbie Hancock-inspired pianist Robert Glasper.

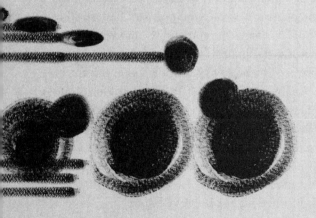

8

JAZZ IN THE FUTURE

It's a fair bet that amid the clamour of jam session cliffhangers, musicians' banter, dubious deals and romances come and gone on the night air in Minton's Playhouse in 1941, none of the beboppers knew or cared that they were at the epicentre of a revolution in 20th-century music. That thought might have been in Thelonious Monk's mind when, years later, he was asked where he thought jazz was headed next. 'I don't know,' he said. 'Maybe it's going to hell'.

Predicting artistic futures is a risky game, but at least back then, jazz evolution had taken a linear path, with the blues, improvisation on popular songs and the vivacity of syncopated rhythms central to everything from New Orleans street music to bebop. In a culturally fragmented new century, such a comparatively straight line may be impossible to follow or predict again. Young players today can now start at any point on contemporary music's compass, and combine just about any element of it with any other one, if they can devise ways of making the disparate elements fit. Digital technology has opened up the jazz vaults to make almost every recorded phrase available at the click of a mouse. Moreover, all the styles of jazz, from ragtime-swung New Orleans polyphony to free-improvisation, are constantly played live all over the world – making all of them contemporary. In such a vast and restless ocean, how can we begin to predict the routes of the next pioneers?

There are perhaps some clues in the ways that today's jazz artists now address that past, and reinvent it for their own era. The American trumpeter and composer Wynton Marsalis, one of the world's most dedicated and charismatically influential defenders of African American jazz history, leads his Lincoln Center Jazz Orchestra on a mission to bring contemporary audiences the live thrill of hearing Armstrong's, Jelly Roll Morton's, Duke Ellington's or Charles Mingus's bands in full cry. Marsalis's neo-classical absorption in the past has made him a controversial figure for some, as he not only protects jazz history and tells the world about it, but he also steers young performers towards treating earlier jazz dialects as essential parts of their equipment, when some might prefer to compile their sources in other ways. But some of them will creatively use those tools in ways neither Marsalis nor any other guide could have imagined.

Wynton Marsalis nourishes respect for the jazz tradition by respecting the methods of the pioneers. So have other traditionalists, though some of them more informally. Glam-rock icon Bryan Ferry released an album of 1970s' Roxy Music hits in 2012 with jazz arrangements modelled on Duke Ellington's early Cotton Club music. In 2011, a 28-year-old Amy Winehouse, in the last months of her life, eloquently showed her jazz roots in a duet on 'Body and Soul' with the 85-year-old star singer Tony Bennett. The acclaimed American pianist and composer Jason Moran recently reinvented the 1930s' hits of

Fats Waller as a mixture of cutting-edge jazz, dark contemporary parables and 21st-century R&B. The hugely popular work of Diana Krall, the mainstream singer-pianist, constantly reflects the influences of personal mentors such as Ella Fitzgerald's bass partner Ray Brown, and former Billie Holiday pianist Jimmy Rowles.

The jazz tradition, then, seems in good hands – on the concert stages, and increasingly in the programmes of formerly all-classical music-schools. But this is not the whole story of jazz today, and many contemporary players devote their lives to stretching the envelope with the same fearless and fascinated curiosity that drove Louis Armstrong with the Hot Fives, Duke Ellington at the Cotton Club, Charlie Parker and Dizzy Gillespie in 1940s' Harlem, or Ornette Coleman walking the improvising highwire of harmolodics.

New sounds and grooves are audible everywhere, bringing younger audiences and performers for whom the songs of the Gershwins or the feel of a 4/4 swing beat represent a receding culture. The loops and cycles of computer music, contemporary-classical minimalist techniques, the tightly interlocking drum patterns of hip-hop, metrical structures drawn from African and Asian traditions – these and many other new ingredients are going into the jazz mix. Sometimes the familiar identifying marks of earlier jazz – blues inflections, bebop melodies, walking basslines, swing drumming – are evident, sometimes they're barely audible or absent. But jazz as an *attitude* rather than a style or collection of techniques continues to permeate contemporary music. In the loop-like themes of American saxophonists Steve Coleman or Tim Berne, in jazz/hip-hop pianist Robert Glasper's widely popular work, in John Zorn's scorching fusions of free-jazz, contemporary-classical structures and Jewish traditional song, in Steve Lehman's mix of laterally-swinging jazz and compositions inspired by computer-music, and in composer Maria Schneider's clouds of orchestral sound, the jazz spirit burns on.

Meanwhile crowds will groove shoulder to shoulder in packed venues for an ensemble such as Norway's eclectic Jaga Jazzist, as much entranced by the visceral appeal of thundering drums and raucous, anthemic melodies as they had been in the New Orleans dance halls a century earlier.

As Max Roach said, 'jazz allows you to be what you are – to sound 20 when you're 20, and 50 when you're 50'.

As a musical art driven as much or more by its players than by the top-down edicts of composers, jazz constantly evolves, even if there are periods when it seems to be dormant. Throughout the world, the jazz tradition has helped to liberate the individual musician's capacity for self-expression. The process goes on. New angles on music-making, influenced by jazz intonation and improvisation, but also by the world's many other lines of musical force, are forming what 'jazz' – that quintessential, humanely imperfectible work-in-progress – is always becoming.

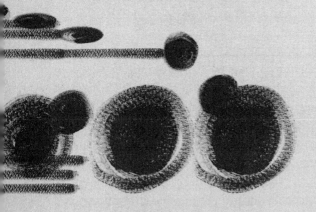

9
A GUIDE TO JAZZ-SPEAK

Jazz has sometimes seemed like a mysterious dark art to those outside its loop – an impression reinforced by its private language. Here is a short lexicon of jazz jargon.

ACID JAZZ

When jazz returned to dance-floor popularity in the late 1980s and early '90s – largely through a revival of interest in 1960s' soul jazz and hard-bop styles – this term was coined to describe the phenomenon by fans and DJs.

BEBOP/REBOP/BOP

Onomatopoeic name derived from rhythmically sung nonsense syllables, to describe the complex, fast-moving new jazz style developed in the 1940s as a reaction – led by Charlie Parker, Dizzy Gillespie and others – against commercial swing music.

BLUES

Originally a singing style with early African American roots (later adapted as a staple form for jazz instrumental music too) developed principally as a 12-bar structure from the early 1900s, and frequently using alterations or slurs to the third and seventh notes of a conventional scale.

BOOGIE-WOOGIE

Blues-based piano style developed in the early 20th century, based on a highly rhythmic, repeated bass line. Later influenced the development of guitar accompaniments in rock and roll.

CHANGES

When jazz musicians refer to 'playing the changes', they mean improvising on the related notes of a song's chord sequence. A crucial underpinning of swing and bebop jazz styles.

CIRCULAR BREATHING

A difficult technique, mostly used by saxophonists, for inhaling air through the nose whilst simultaneously expelling it through the instrument – which allows long passages to be executed without pauses.

COOL SCHOOL

A quieter and more reflective way of playing jazz, developed in the late 1940s as a reaction against the intensity of bebop. Trumpeter Miles Davis and pianist Lennie Tristano were among its instigators and popular variations on it were performed by pianist Dave Brubeck, trumpeter Chet Baker, the Modern Jazz Quartet and many others.

DIXIELAND/TRAD JAZZ

A 1940s' revival of interest in the music of the first jazz pioneers, with New Orleans musicians Willie Gary 'Bunk' Johnson and Edward 'Kid' Ory returning to the spotlight, and many professional and amateur musicians around the world copying the style in the 1950s.

FREE JAZZ

In the late 1950s, and extensively in the following decade, adventurous jazz musicians sought ways of playing intuitively together without dependence on regular song chords and sometimes without regular rhythms or grooves too. Saxophonist John Coltrane and Ornette Coleman were key figures in this movement, which spawned local variations around the world.

FUNK

A word originally denoting pungent smells, and adapted as a description of earthy, often blues-derived music. It became identified with a style of danceable, rock-influenced jazz in the 1950s.

FUSION

Often used interchangeably with jazz-rock to describe various syntheses of jazz, soul, pop, funk and rock music that began to emerge in the mid-1970s.

FAKE BOOK

A collection of musical scores detailing the melodies and chord-structures of standard songs, pop hits and widely used jazz themes. Fake books have frequently been informal collections, distributed privately, because the music they contain is often still bound by copyright laws.

HARMOLODICS

Saxophonist Ornette Coleman's term for a collectively improvising process in which the melody, harmony and rhythm of a piece are being simultaneously transformed by all the performers in real time.

HEAD

A song's theme or main melody. Jazz musicians can move a long way from the tune or starting point in the course of an improvisation, and when bandleaders point to their heads, it's a signal to move back to the original song.

LICKS

Familiar improvisers' phrases, sometimes fallen back on in the course of a solo to give the performer time to consider new avenues, and sometimes to draw a welcoming reaction from the audience.

MAINSTREAM

The name given to jazz reflecting the 1930s' swing era sound, played by surviving swing veterans and their admirers from the 1950s onwards.

MODAL JAZZ

Largely instigated by the researches of composer George Russell in the 1950s, modal jazz used cycles of scale-like patterns or modes as an open and spacious basis for improvising, rather than the more rigid structures of chord progressions. Miles Davis's 1959 album 'Kind of Blue' is the most famous example of the style.

MULTIPHONICS

Though most wind instruments were designed to play one note at a time, jazz musicians, including the saxophonists Illinois Jacquet and John Coltrane, used alternative fingering and blowing techniques to sound several notes simultaneously in chord-like effects.

POST BOP

Catch-all term often used to group together jazz made from the 1980s onwards, where there are detectable references to bebop melodies and rhythms, though input from later developments such as free jazz and jazz funk or soul music may also be present.

RAGTIME

A popular dance style of the late 1890s and early 1900s, based on 'ragging' of the rhythm so that emphases are shifted from normal strong beats to weak ones, in a syncopation technique giving an exciting skip or kick to the pulse. Ragtime forms were significant inspirations to early jazz melodies and rhythms.

RIFF

A repeated figure, often harmonised between several players or an orchestral section, to act as sharply accented accompaniment to an improvising soloist.

SCAT

Vocal style often used by jazz singers, in which the characteristic phrasing of an instrumental solo is mimicked by the voice. Louis Armstrong was a scat pioneer, though the technique had been used earlier in vaudeville and comedy routines.

STANDARD

Abbreviation of 'standard song', which usually meant – during the swing era and subsequently – a Tin Pan Alley or Broadway hit song used as a vehicle for jazz. Impromptu jam sessions often rely on 'standards' whose chord progressions are widely shared by players.

STRIDE

A development of the original ragtime-piano method, in which the left hand plays a strongly rhythmic pattern alternating with single bass notes, octaves and chords. The 'stride school' centred on New York in the 1920s, with James P. Johnson and Fats Waller among its leading exponents. Art Tatum brought an unprecedented virtuosity to the approach.

SWING

An elusive jazz concept, because it involves sustaining the impression of a steady, usually four-beat, rhythm, whilst superimposing phrases that make it feel looser and more supple, by fine adjustments to the placing of notes and the timing of accents.

THIRD STREAM

A term coined by the musicologist and composer Gunther Schuller in the 1950s to describe crossover experiments in which the methods of classical composers and jazz composer/improvisers are joined.

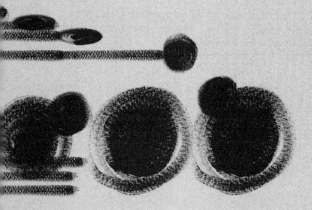

10 WHY THEY MATTERED – RECORDINGS AND INFLUENCES

NEW ORLEANS

BUDDY BOLDEN

Check out: A wax cylinder recording by Bolden's band is rumoured to have been made, but never found.
Influence: Leading New Orleans cornetist from late 1890s to 1907, joined the rhythms of ragtime to an emotional blues sound.

JELLY ROLL MORTON

Check out: 'King Porter Stomp', 1923; 'The Pearls', 1923; Library of Congress Recordings, 1938.
Influence: Infused ragtime with Hispanic rhythms, used multiple instruments in sections to enable some of the earliest jazz arrangements.

SIDNEY BECHET

Check out: 'Sweetie Dear', 1932; 'Summertime', 1939; 'Petite Fleur', 1952.
Influence: On the phrasing of saxophone improvisation, and the sound of soprano saxophonists in the instrument's resurgence in the 1960s.

LOUIS ARMSTRONG

Check out: Hot Fives and Hot Sevens, 1925–1929; 'Satch Plays Fats', 1955; 'What A Wonderful World', 1967.
Influence: Pioneered the virtuosic improvised jazz solo; developed phrasing that inspired players of many instruments, and the writing of ensemble parts; originated a vocal style influencing singers from Billie Holiday to Tom Waits.

BIX BEIDERBECKE

Check out: 'Royal Garden Blues', 1927; 'Singin' The Blues', 1927; 'In A Mist', 1927.
Influence: Inspired many early brass-players including Rex Stewart and Bunny Berigan, brought unconventional harmonies to jazz – and was an inspiration to the late 1940s 'Cool School'.

SWING

FLETCHER HENDERSON/ DON REDMAN

Check out: 'Dicty Blues', 1923; 'Sugar Foot Stomp', 1924.
Influence: Phrased big-band scores like 'hot' jazz solos, inspired many swing bandleaders.

DUKE ELLINGTON

Check out: 'The Mooche', 1928; 'Sophisticated Lady', 1932; 'Harlem Airshaft', 1940.
Influence: Used the whole orchestra as his instrument, creatively balanced composition and the idiosyncrasies of his favourite soloists.

COUNT BASIE

Check out: 'One O' Clock Jump', 1937; 'Jumpin' at the Woodside', 1938; 'Taxi War Dance', 1939.
Influence: Gave four-beat swing rhythms an infectious buoyancy, emphasised the blues, and the ensemble accompaniment of riffs.

BENNY GOODMAN

Check out: 'Stompin' at the Savoy', 1936; 'Sing Sing Sing', 1937.
Influence: Brought authentic jazz to a wide audience for listening and dancing, combined exciting arrangements, gifted soloists and meticulous discipline.

BESSIE SMITH

Check out: 'Down Hearted Blues', 1923; 'St Louis Blues', 1925; 'Nobody wants you when you're down and out', 1925.
Influence: Gave the blues an operatic power, used instrument-like effects in intonation, transformed the emotional scope of popular songs.

COLEMAN HAWKINS

Check out: 'Dicty Blues' (with Fletcher Henderson), 1923; 'Body and Soul', 1939; 'Picasso' (unaccompanied), 1948.
Influence: Founding father of jazz on the tenor saxophone,

improvised on chords as well as melodies, paved the way for Sonny Rollins, John Coltrane and other tenor-sax stars.

LESTER YOUNG

Check out: 'Lady Be Good', 'Shoe Shine Boy', 1936; 'Lester Leaps In', 1939.
Influence: A key inspiration for Charlie Parker, but also on the Cool School saxophonists.

ELLA FITZGERALD

Check out: 'A-Tisket A-Tasket', 1938; 'Flying Home', 1945; 'The George and Ira Gershwin Song Book', 1959.
Influence: On the phrasing and timing of innumerable jazz and popular singers around the world, from the 1950s to today.

BILLIE HOLIDAY

Check out: 'Why Was I Born?', 1937; 'Strange Fruit', 1939.
Influence: Inspiration to many jazz singers, raised the stature of jazz vocalists to equality with the best instrumentalists.

BEBOP AND POST-SWING

CHARLIE CHRISTIAN

Check out: 'Flying Home', 'Seven Come Eleven', 1939.
Influence: Made the electric guitar a soloist's instrument, influenced bebop thinking, particularly rhythmically.

KENNY CLARKE

Check out: 'One Bass Hit', 1946; 'Solar' (with Miles Davis), 1954.
Influence: Bebop co-founder, crucial to loosening and lightening jazz drummers' methods.

MILES DAVIS

Check out: 'Billie's Bounce', 1945; 'Budo', 1949; 'Dig', 1951; 'So What', 1959; 'Miles Runs The Voodoo Down', 1969; 'Right Off', 1970; 'Human Nature', 1985.
Influence: One of the most charismatic and widely-copied of all jazz musicians, for his trumpet sound and ensemble approach. Made bebop more spacious, later explored modal jazz, orchestral jazz and funk.

DIZZY GILLESPIE

Check out: 'Salt Peanuts', 1945; 'A Night in Tunisia', 1946; 'Cubana Be-Cubana Bop', 1947.
Influence: Harmonically advanced bebop innovator, star trumpet virtuoso.

THELONIOUS MONK

Check out: 'Round Midnight', 1947; 'Little Rootie Tootie', 1954; 'Blue Monk', 1954; 'Brilliant Corners', 1956.
Influence: Piano-style replaced bebop's fast lines with percussive chords and dissonance, much-interpreted unique composer.

CHARLIE PARKER

Check out: 'Now's The Time', 'Koko', 1945; 'Yardbird Suite', 1946.
Influence: Brilliant musical mind, and leading catalyst to the mid 20th century creative upheaval of bebop. Liberated improvisation on chord structures, dominated agenda of post-World War II jazz.

MAX ROACH

Check out: 'Koko' (with Charlie Parker), 1945; 'I'll Remember April' (with Bud Powell), 1947.
Influence: Roach loosened drummers' dictatorial beat, accompanied the unfolding ideas of improvisers in more reactive ways.

COOL TO FREE

MODERN JAZZ QUARTET

Check out: 'Django', 1954; 'Bags' Groove', 1957; 'The Golden Striker', 1957.
Influence: Successfully fused bebop improvising methods, blues, European counterpoint techniques and Cool School restraint, produced several popular jazz themes.

LENNIE TRISTANO

Check out: 'Intuition', 1949; 'Requiem', 1955.
Influence: Showed that advanced melodic improvising could be just as expressive as more obviously emotive jazz methods. In relaxing the dictates of chord progressions, he was also a discreet pioneer of free jazz.

DAVE BRUBECK

Check out: 'Balcony Rock', 1954; 'Blue Rondo A La Turk', 1959; 'Take Five', 1959.
Influence: Showed complex time signatures could work in jazz without hampering improvisation or swing. Crucial jazz populist who nonetheless never compromised artistic quality.

BILL EVANS

Check out: 'Waltz for Debby', 1956; 'Peace Piece', 1958; 'Turn Out The Stars', 1967.
Influence: 'The Chopin of jazz piano', Evans was a sophisticated romantic with a delicate touch, who inspired many star pianists, including McCoy Tyner, Keith Jarrett and Brad Mehldau.

CHET BAKER

Check out: 'My Funny Valentine', 1952.
Influence: One of the iconic figures of the Cool School for both his sound and his image – a soft-toned trumpeter who did more with less.

GIL EVANS

Check out: 'La Nevada', 1960; 'Hotel Me', 1963; 'Las Vegas Tango', 1964.
Influence: A big-ensemble composing inspiration almost as significant as Duke Ellington, who introduced tone colours and instrumentation rarely used in jazz before.

JAZZ MESSENGERS

Check out: 'Moanin'', 1959; 'A Night In Tunisia', 1960.
Influence: A model for hard bop bands in the mixing of gospel phrasing and rhythms with bop swing – and the most significant jazz finishing school of the 1960s to the '90s, with many budding stars featuring in Blakey's line-ups.

SONNY ROLLINS

Check out: 'Blue Seven', 1957; 'Softly As In A Morning Sunrise', 1957.
Influence: A model for post-war tenor saxophonists, for his absorption of both 1930s' swing and bebop methods.

ORNETTE COLEMAN

Check out: 'Ramblin'', 1958; 'Lonely Woman', 1959; 'Morning Song', 1965; 'Dancing In Your Head', 1975.
Influence: Transformed how small-band improvisation could work, by relinquishing song forms based on chords and encouraging spontaneous conversations around shifting tonal centres and responsive drumming and bass-playing.

JOHN COLTRANE

Check out: 'Giant Steps', 1959; 'My Favourite Things', 1960; 'Impressions', 1963; 'A Love Supreme', 1964.
Influence: Radically expanded saxophone possibilities beyond the instrument's designed range, developed multiphonic techniques to permit saxophone chords, evolved ensemble approaches for small and large groups.

CECIL TAYLOR

Check out: 'Bemsha Swing', 1956; 'D Trad, That's What', 1962; 'The Tree Of Life', 1991.
Influence: Offered a dramatic alternative to bebop-steered piano jazz – with classical and jazz phrasing compressed into marathon high-energy solos and a hard-hitting, percussive attack.

GEORGE RUSSELL

Check out: 'Round Johnny Rondo', 1956; 'Concerto For Billy The Kid', 1956; 'Dimensions', 1960.
Influence: A free-thinking composer whose revolutionary concepts of harmony, modalism and rhythm influenced soloists (including Miles Davis, Ornette Coleman and Jan Garbarek), small groups and big bands.

SUN RA

Check out: 'Blues At Midnight', 1958; 'When Angels Speak Of Love', 1963; 'Prelude To Stargazers', 1990.

Influence: A complete one-off as a musician and a human being, he made old Swing Era music sound *avant-garde*, brought theatrical and dance elements to big-band jazz performance, and did much to turn the Moog synthesiser into a solo jazz instrument.

FUSION AND CONTEMPORARY

JOE ZAWINUL

Check out: 'Mercy, Mercy, Mercy', 1966; 'In a Silent Way', 1969; 'Birdland', 1977.
Influence: Greatly enlarged the synthesiser's jazz vocabulary, raised the bar for jazz-fusion and world-music through Weather Report and the Zawinul Syndicate.

PAT METHENY

Check out: 'Are You Going With Me?', 1981; 'Rejoicing', 1983; 'Police People', 1985; 'Follow Me', 1997.
Influence: A highly personal guitarist mixing jazz spontaneity and finesse with song-like accessibility.

HERBIE HANCOCK

Check out: 'Watermelon Man', 1962; 'Maiden Voyage', 1964; 'Dolphin Dance', 1964; 'Chameleon', 1973.
Influence: Showed musicians from all genres how jazz thinking could liberate their work, whatever its roots. Opened pop and rock audiences to jazz methods. Much-copied piano stylist.

JOHN MCLAUGHLIN

Check out: 'Binky's Beam', 1969; 'Meeting Of The Spirits', 1971; 'Joy', 1976.
Influence: Set new standards for guitar improvisation, built bridges between Eastern and Western traditions.

JAN GARBAREK

Check out: 'Dis', 1976; 'Witchi-Tai-To', 1993; 'Officium', 1998.
Influence: Gave jazz saxophonists ambient alternatives to post-Coltrane intensity, encouraged jazz/classical crossover through the 'Officium' project.

CARLA BLEY

Check out: 'Ida Lupino', 1965; 'Mother Of The Dead Man', 1967; 'The Star Spangled

Banner', 2002; 'The Lost Chords', 2003.
Influence: An inheritor of the jazz-composing legacies of Gil Evans and Duke Ellington, Bley has given those traditions influential new meanings through her stylistic eclecticism.

___

WAYNE SHORTER

Check out: 'Dance Cadaverous', 1964; 'Infant Eyes', 1964; 'Footprints', 1966.
Influence: As a Coltrane- and Sonny Rollins-inspired saxophonist who offered new routes beyond the dominance of both, and as a jazz composer whose pieces broke the tradition's moulds but still sounded deeply rooted in jazz practice.

___

KEITH JARRETT

Check out: 'Gypsy Moth', 1971; 'The Köln Concert', 1975; 'Blackbird, Bye Bye', 1991; 'The Carnegie Hall Concert', 2005.
Influence: Developed widely imitated blend of post-bop jazz, classical phrasing and gospel rhythms for piano improvisers, and became a widely admired model for contemporary small ensemble jazz with his American and European quartets of the 1970s.

___

BILL FRISELL

Check out: 'The Open Prairie', 1993; 'Shenandoah', 1999.
Influence: A brilliant adapter of electronic effects to jazz and improv ends, and a unique cherisher of the sounds of American life.

___

ABDULLAH IBRAHIM

Check out: 'Tintiyana', 1965; 'Mannenberg', 1974; 'Water From An Ancient Well', 1986.
Influence: The introduction, to western ears, of a new palette of references for jazz improvisation, coming from African choral music and fusions of American jazz with the *marabi* and *kwela* dance styles of the South African townships.

KENNY WHEELER

Check out: 'Everybody's Song But My Own', 1987; 'Opening', 1990; 'Angel Song', 1995.
Influence: Joined a Cool School trumpet sound to free-improvisations; combined Gil Evans' composing methods with classical influences such as Paul Hindemith's.

ESBJÖRN SVENSSON

Check out: 'Dodge The Dodo', 1998; 'Good Morning Susie Soho', 2000.
Influence: The adaptation of a Keith Jarrett-inspired take on the sound of the jazz-piano trio to a contemporary music world of funk, hip-hop and theatrically dramatic performance.

WYNTON MARSALIS

Check out: 'Much Later', 1985; 'Dead Man Blues', 1993; 'Stardust', 2003.
Influence: Turned a young generation onto jazz in the 1980s, demonstrated to the world the live impact of jazz groundbreakers otherwise only heard on record, and increasingly now brings non-American perceptions of jazz under the prestigious Lincoln Center umbrella.

INDEX

ACKNOWLEDGEMENTS

Thanks to *The Guardian* and to *Jazz on 3* for giving me the space, time and means to pursue such a bewitching subject – and to Ron Atkins, Nigel Fountain, Val Wilmer, Jez Nelson and Richard Williams, among many colleagues and friends, who have helped deepen my understanding of it. Thanks also to Jane O'Shea and Romilly Morgan at Quadrille for keeping such steady hands on the wheel, and to Alison Cathie for steering me in their direction. Extra special thanks, as ever, to Ros, Fred and Leo – for their advice, wit, wisdom and patience beyond the call.